How I Produced A Movie With Eight Thousand Dollars

by

Sandra L. LaVaughn

LaVauri Publishing House

How I Produced A Movie With Eight Thousand Dollars
Copyright 2009 by Sandra L. LaVaughn

Revised edition 2020

Published by LaVauri Publishing House
Printed in the United States of America

For more information visit my website at:
www.lavonproductions.com

Acknowledgements

I dedicate this book to my Lord and Savior Jesus Christ who is always there leading and guiding me in the right directions.

To my children Ricky R. LaVaughn, my first-born and editor of this book, to Esther L. Madison my daughter the accountant and encourager. Thank you both for being wonderful children.

To my daughter's husband Robert Madison, thank you for joining our little family and helping with the family businesses.

Many thanks to my uncle John Word, who is no longer with us; he was my advisor and the monarch of the Word family. To, my ninety-year-old cousin, Curley Reynolds, who still cuts the grass, paint the house, cook delicious food, and drive anywhere she pleases, your healthy longevity and gentle kindness is my inspiration.

I love you all.

Table of Contents

Prologue	**	5
Chapter One	Pre-Production *****************************	10
Chapter Two	Production **********************************	14
Chapter Three	Post-Production *****************************	21
Chapter Four	How I Produced A Movie With Eight Thousand dollars ****	25
Chapter Five	The Blue Room Screenplay ************************	31
Chapter Six	Scene 1 **************************************	114
	Scene 2 **************************************	119
	Scene 3 **************************************	128
	Scene 4 **************************************	133
	Scene 5 **************************************	136
Chapter Seven	Scene Chart **********************************	138
	Main Actor Call Sheet *************************	139
	Character Scene Number ***********************	141
	Initial Shooting Schedule **********************	142
	Time Shooting Schedule ***********************	143
	Main Scene Locations **************************	144
	Wardrobe Chart ******************************	144

PROLOGUE

Filming *The Blue Room* was an exciting adventure, and a great learning experience. Film schools, workshops, and reading mountains of books is a necessary education, however, the real training is on the job. Unfortunate mishaps are bound to happen while filming, hence the combination of on the job training, education, and quick thinking to devise a solution is the repairer of the issue.

I spent several years trying to sale one script. Then a thought kicked in, write several scripts and sale one of those, I tried for years but only received rejection letters. Yet it took a single night to come to the decision that I would produce, write, and finance a movie. This book is about my journey from scriptwriter to film producer and director. I did it because I had to move forward and stop depending on someone else and making excuses.

September of 1990, I became a divorced mother with two small children. Ricky was eleven, and Esther nine years old. In 1992, I had a friend who read a few of my poems and one of my stories; she suggested that I put my work on television. I was a surgical nurse and knew nothing about the TV industry. My friend found a number in the phone book (wow that sounds antediluvian) she wrote the number down and handed it to me. Two weeks later, I was taking a three-month course in production, scriptwriting, and directing. After finishing the courses, I produced my first TV show titled *Gun Safety;* the thirty-minute program featured a police officer, a City Councilman, and the moderator. The Councilman believed in having loaded guns in every room, while the officer maintained the subject matter of safety first. He also vehemently reminded the Councilman about Ohio rules and gun regulations. At which time an argument ensued between the two men while the moderator fought to regain control. The director of the show was getting ready to shout, "Cut", I grabbed her arm and whispered, "Let'em have at it."

The confrontation added excitement, controversy, and more viewers. Editing was a blast. *Gun Safety* was nominated for the Pyramid Award. I was hooked; after that show I took editing classes.

A few months later an incident nearly caused me to leave the industry, but the challenge of hiring the crew and actors, planning the budget, choosing locations, production meetings, and pondering over the script was in my blood. One evening the crew, the spokesperson, and myself was at the TV station waiting on the director. We were shooting a commercial for a local church that was having a special occasion, the director was nowhere to be found; all eyes were on me.

Hum, what to do? I simply jumped in with unsteady feet and directed the show. Perspiration rolled from the roots of my hair all the way down to the arch in my feet. To this day, I am very thankful that the evenings schedule was light. It is funny how things work out. During the time I was learning how to direct I didn't like it. Then a simple no show caused an unseen passion buried some place deep inside to emerge. A few days later the director called to apologize, her apology was accepted. Honestly, thanks to her from that point on I directed my programs as well as other producers.

Still, I could not sale a script so I prayed asking the lord to let a Studio or Production Company be interested. In 1994, He answered my prayers. A friend introduced me to the author of the book titled, *Why Didn't I Think of That*, he was also friends with a Hollywood producer. The author read the script first, and then mailed it to the producer. Both men love the story's concept. The producer wanted us to make a few changes and add more action. The author wanted to talk over the phone everyday to make the changes according to the producer's request. They could have tweak the story just enough so that it was no longer my story. They did not.

The author called suggesting that we kill off a few of the characters. Though God had opened the door of opportunity, I slammed it shut during the first phone call. I told him to leave the script as is because I did not want to kill any of the characters. Unfortunately, he never called again. An answered prayer fizzled and returned unused.

Discouragement took over I gave up and decided that I would never make it in the industry. Were those days gone forever? It appeared so. I walked around with my head held high and a fake smile plastered on my face. Because of the children I existed under the facade that all was well, fortunately practicing to be happy became a reality.

Years later, I rewrote the script; can you guess what I did? Yep, I added action, death, and a new twist for the escape. The original story was unique, interesting, but dull and badly in need of a polish. The author and Hollywood producer knew this I chose not to listen. In the nineties I was young, a know it all, and not nearly as wise or smart as I thought.

By 2000, both of my children were students at The Ohio State University. One evening in January, Ricky called and said that an actor, who was on Love Boat, was on campus performing a one-man play about Paul Lawrence Dunbar. Mr. Dunbar from Dayton, Ohio, was a Black American writer who lived during the early 1900's. Ricky gave me the producer of the play phone number. Dare I try again? The answer was an unsure yes. I called the producer and in turn, she got me in contact with the actor. What joy, a little piece of Hollywood here in Columbus, and I was talking with him. I should say I stammered, stuttered, and sputtered words that fell clumsily out of my mouth. Nevertheless, I took him to the Martin Luther King Breakfast where we talked and ate. By the end of the breakfast and the program, he agreed to direct the documentary that I was researching.

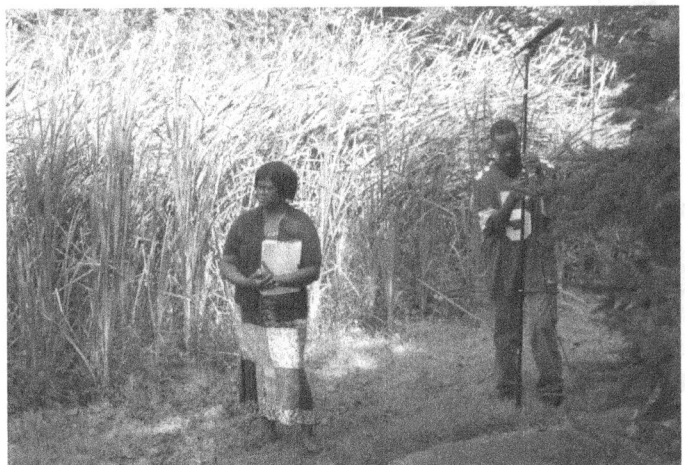

Producer/Director (Sandra) and Assistant Director (Ricky) discussing the scene.

With the help of a grant writer, I got busy and began writing several grants asking for development, production, and preproduction funds. Each grantor replied saying the history is imprecise. The Board agreed that my research and findings was accurate, but the truth would unravel a lie that permeate two prominent American families from the past, and humiliate their off springs that remain to live within the realm of the deception. Needless to say, I did not get the money. The dishonesty continues to be taught in American schools from elementary through college. It is my plan to untangle the thick mesh of falsehoods by filming the truth to correct a small portion of American history.

In 2004, I mailed the revised script that the author and producer liked to Sony Studio, just on a whim. WOW! An employee at the Studio called, he asked me to fax the synopsis and budget. I was asking for eleven million; I thought they would send me a nice rejection letter. Six weeks later, Matt from Sony called stating a couple of the producers wanted me to shoot a small fragment of the script; he said they liked the story. I said, "Okay," but failed to follow through because of the lack of money. Years later, I learned that Warner Brothers asked the same request of the producer who shot *300*. He got the money together and shot a few minutes of a fight scene. His script was funded. Thus, I had made another serious blunder. I never gave Sony a chance to say that they were going to produce the script, or send a denial letter. Simply, I will always wonder what would have been the outcome.

"Sometimes God comes when you want Him," but if we're not paying attention, we miss out on the blessing. Then say, "But He's always on time."

In 2001, Ricky wrote his first book while a junior at The Ohio State University, the book title, "When Roses Cry," the publisher was Publish America. Six years later Esther began her PH D program. One evening, June 2006, Ricky and I were visiting Esther, we reminisced about the good old days, calling studios, producers, and receiving rejection letters from famous people. I had learned form my errors and could laugh about them. As we were laughing and talking, a thought popped into my head. I blurted out, "let's shoot a movie, I'll fund the project." I had several stories and scripts written, but they were too expensive for me to produce. Ideas whirled around the walls of our minds when Ricky softly, almost to himself said, *"The Blue Room."* He had no story, only a title based off the blue walls in Esther's living room.

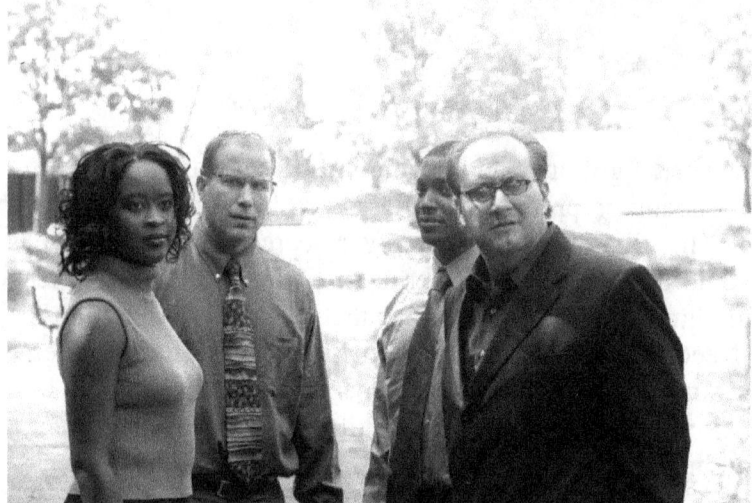

This scene was shot early in the morning on the first day of film shoot. (Esther, Ned, Anthony, John) During the scene a bug flew into Anthony's eye, he was cool, calm, and collected and said not a word. None of us knew about the bug until I yelled, "cut."

From the title, we hashed out a rough draft about three desperate businessmen who kidnapped themselves for ransom. When Sony asked me to shoot a short, I had a job, and a little money saved. Shooting *"The Blue Room,"* I had a job, and a little money saved.

Good grief, déjà vu.

I was given a third chance this time without the backing of a studio or producer, it did not matter because I was happy for the opportunity. I jumped in with a loud, "I AM LISTENING."

The door was not locked.

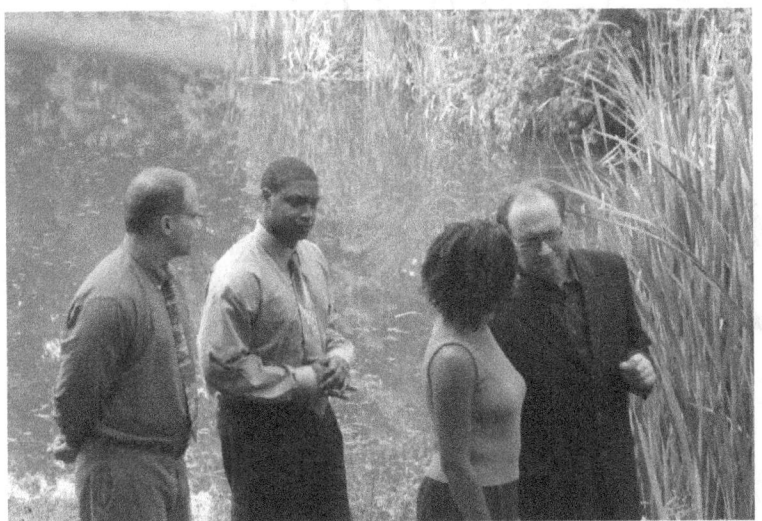
Ned, Anthony, Esther, and John – the plot thickens.

CHAPTER ONE

PRE-PRODUCTION

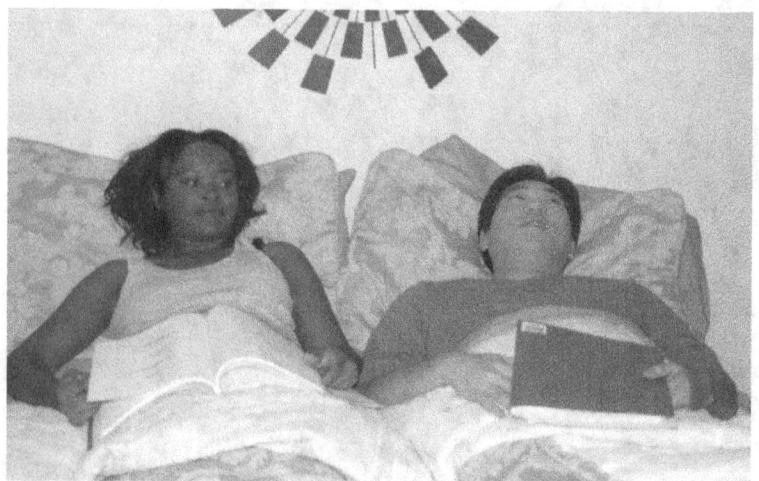

Esther and David are reviewing their parts. Although this is not a love scene, still the actors were uncomfortable, for good reason the scene was shot after lunch, in bed, on the first day. The actors were gallant and played their part magnificently in spite of it all.

The challenge to shoot a featured-length film within eight days was an audacious decision. I spoke with a professor at Ohio University asking if he knew a director of photographer. He suggested a graduate student, who was working as an intern on a production in New York. The student profoundly told me that it was impossible and no one could shoot a full-length film in less than four weeks. To expound upon this notion he sent a three-page single space email explaining how and why it was not possible. I deleted his email. If I finished in eight days great, if extra days were needed no problem. My failure would be in doing nothing, so I pressed on.

A few of my co-workers were encouraging, the rest were vehemently critical. They told me to "stick with the job at hand," or "you have a good job, what is wrong with you?" Gotta' love this one "Who do you think you are, a female Spike Lee?" My all time favorite, "you will never make it in *those* people world." Their dogmatic discouraging words could have sunk my dream and extinguished an answered prayer into the abyss of nothingness. I was determined.

My search for a film crew began by contacting the Columbus Film Commission; they were in the process of growing, their list was none existing. My first quest was to find a director of photography (DP). I called the Columbus College of Arts, which was helpful. They gave me the name of a recent graduate. He did not feel comfortable due to his lack of experience, so he gave me the name of a person who was an experienced camera operator. Sadly, he was on his way to Europe. My search continued. To my surprise, before leaving America, he sent me an email saying to ask his friend. I immediately sent his friend an email; he accepted the position as the DP, in addition, he brought with him the majority of the crew. I got the gaffer, still photographer, and the hair and makeup artist. They all agreed to work from the back end.

It took planning, a small miracle, hardworking crew, and actors, to shoot a ninety-minute film with $8,000.000. There was not enough money for tryouts or interviews or studio rental, instead I had readings in my home. Most of the actors were friends and family. David Lim was from a Talent Agency located in Ohio. Ned Lynch was and still is a Broadway actor living in New York City, his acting skills were phenomenal.

The characters of Sparrow, Lisa, and Cole were painstakingly difficult to find, but the remaining actors were hired from the first reading.

Six weeks before shooting, we had the first reading. John Michael decided his character Chandler Vilderman should have a British accent. Ricky LaVaughn as Detective Vince wore the bolo as his signature. Ned called and shared his vision for his character who was a neurotic coffee drinker; he added glasses and a face twitch. Five weeks from filming the woman playing Sparrow moved to California. At the first reading, the person chosen to play Cole was lacking the necessary reading skills. I thought, "Oh my goodness how do I tell this man he can't play the part."

Cole was not the major character his part however, was major and very important to the plot.

The next day he removed himself by stating he was busy with his son's soccer team. I was saved. The first woman who read for Lisa's character had an ill husband, so she stayed home to take care of him. Lisa's character was talkative and over the top perky, the woman who read the part was serious and homely. I was sorry about her husband's illness, but again saved.

It did not take long to find Cole, I asked a co-worker, who was 6'5." He had a music duplication company, plus he wanted to be an actor. He could read, handsome, clean cut, had his own business, and a desire to be an actor. Perfect. Through a talent agency we found the second Lisa, she too was perfect. She was blonde and ditzy her reading was wonderful

By the fourth week, we still did not have Sparrow; it was looking like production was going to be delayed yet I continued forward.

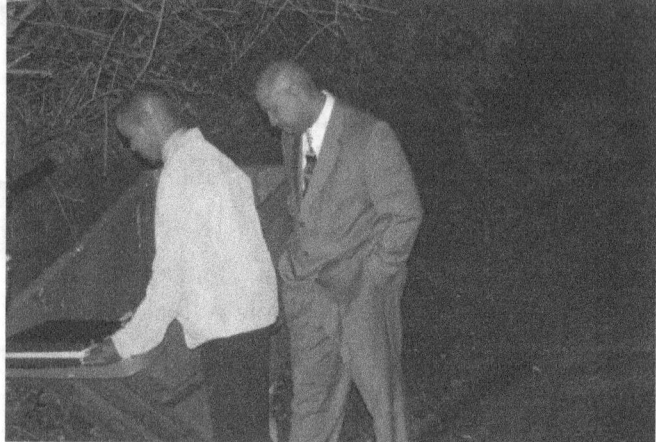

Ricky and Bill, as the two detectives find a mysterious note in the briefcase. One of them was an informant for the bad guys.

My prayers intensified. I called the actors to give them the date and time of the next reading. Sorry to say, the woman playing Lisa phone was disconnected. I mailed her a letter; one week later, it was returned stamped on the envelope was no such address. The only correct contact was her email, which I never received a reply.

Ricky and I began our quest to find another Lisa and continuous search for Sparrow. Then the unthinkable happened. The tall man who accepted the role of Cole Harris backed out, my heart sunk down into the depth of disappointment. As he explained the reason he could not be Cole, there were tears in his eyes, and a quiver in his voice. He passionately wanted to be in the movie and write two songs. His wife, on the other hand, told him that he did not have time. A few weeks later, he gave up his city job to work for Wal-Mart and moved his office in his basement. Changing the company's location to his home forced him to lay off his two employees. After production, I called to check on him, his voice was thick with sadness as he exclaimed his situation. His music business had diminished, hopes of acting obliterated, he said, "I'm existing."

I've never heard from him again.

Esther had a friend from Cincinnati said he would play the part of Cole. He had a smooth soft velvet voice, on the other hand he was too big, too tall, too street, bad teeth, and unattractive. Cole was a clean-cut professional all-American black executive. We were three weeks from filming so I said okay, but kept praying, Lord

You send Cole. The following week he left without a goodbye. That was a good thing.

Some where during this time common sense should have kicked in saying, "delay," it didn't, I continued the search for Lisa, Cole, and Sparrow.

Eight days before production, Esther and I were driving down West Broad Street. We drove past Veterans Memorial under a bridge where a railroad train was crossing when she said, "I am going to have to be Sparrow."

I almost choked. She had not shown an interest in the industry so I never said much to her about it; she had just started her PH D program getting a degree in Public Policy and Administration Nonprofit Management and Leadership, long title, all the same, I said to her, "you don't have to worry about this; you're busy with homework."

She told me that it was okay. When we reached home, I gave her a copy of the script, the next day she knew her part. Wow. I was impressed Sparrow was the main character. Seven days before production, Ricky contacted a friend from his high school days, Miesha Cannaday to play the Lisa character, and Anthony Henderson accepted the role as Cole; they both were employees of JP Morgan Chase. We had one last reading with all of the actors. Finally, crew and actors were hired. Anthony had the voice and looks. The Lisa character was white, blonde, and ditzy. Miesha was black with blondish braids and ditzy; she took the character to another level.

Crew, actors, film sites, sets, and meal providers were in place, we were ready for production to begin.

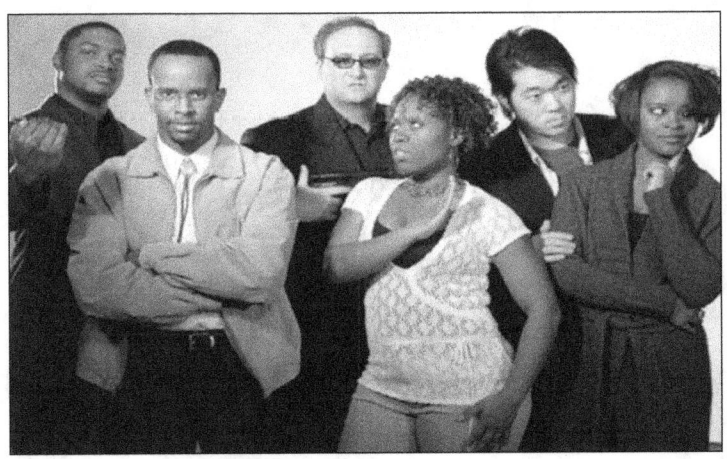

Cast photo for advertising. Those pictured from left to right: Anthony, Ricky, John, Miesha, David, and Esther.

CHAPTER TWO

PRODUCTION

Eight thousand dollars to shoot a full-length movie, edit, and feed over 30 people. What was I thinking? I didn't think, I planned and just did it.

Production began Sunday, September 17, 2006. Most of the crew and all of the hair and makeup artists were from Cleveland, Ohio, Ned Lynch a New York Broadway was from the Big Apple. Everybody arrived Thursday three days before shooting, at which time we had the production meetings. The crew came in with crates and boxes full of equipment. My apartment had two large storage spaces that held everything. When the man from Cincinnati was here, he and Esther had gone shopping for the guns and masks. The guns was black plastic with orange tips, I used a black marker to paint the tips trying to make them look a bit authentic. The set designer brought his guns that looked like the real deal. I showed him the guns that Esther had purchased we had a good laugh. The DP tried to figure out how he could make the shiny plastic objects look real on camera. The set designer told him, "forget about it."

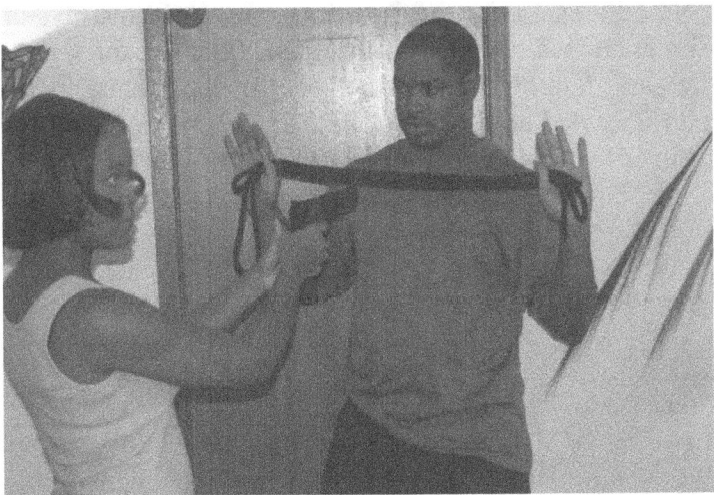

Sparrow (Esther) takes control from Cole (Anthony, they struggled, she get the gun, aimed and accidentally hit his top lip.

Excluding Ned and the crew, the actors and I had day jobs, so when we were not filming on Sundays we filmed weeknights from six p.m. to midnight. We all took off work a few hours early during production.

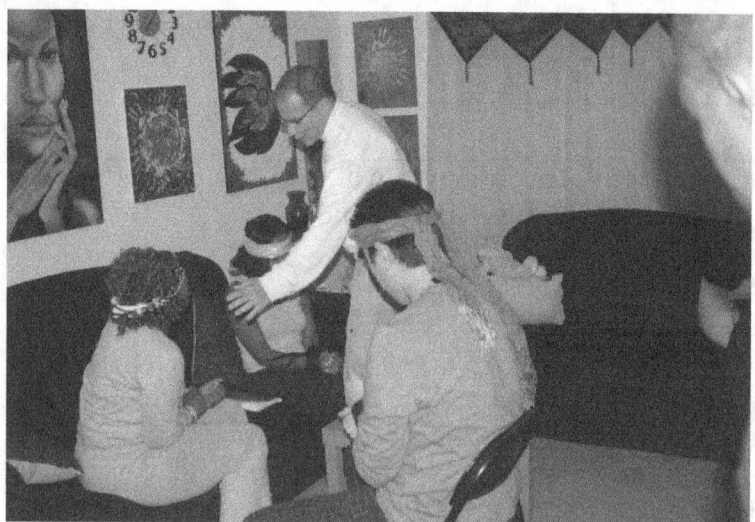

Ned harasses the hostage (Miesha, Esther, and David).

Monday, September 21, 2006, the evening film shoot was an outdoor scene at the O'Shaughnessy Dam. We were shooting the scene where Chandler and Cole tied Zack to a beam and beat him senseless, then left him for the police to find.

The day was cold, cloudy, and raining. I prayed for sunshine, I wanted the rays of the setting sun to sparkle like diamonds dancing on the water. Instead, thick dark gray clouds hovered over the park, rain hit the sides and roof of the shelter house, and the deep sound of thunder growled across the sky. The atmosphere made the scene eerie. For the first time ever I was glad my prayer was not answered.

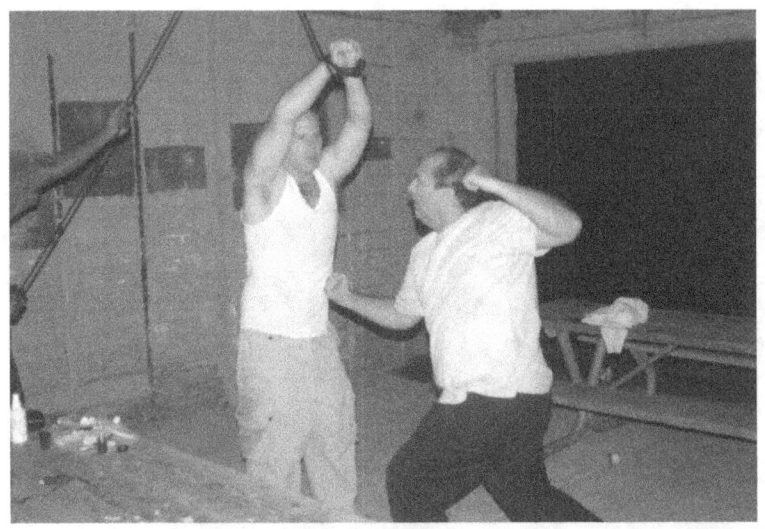

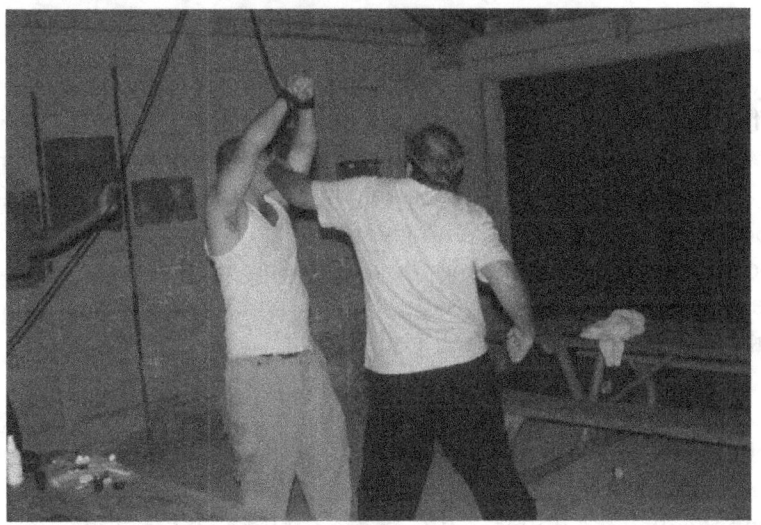

Anthony is holding the rope while John uses Ned for a punching bag.

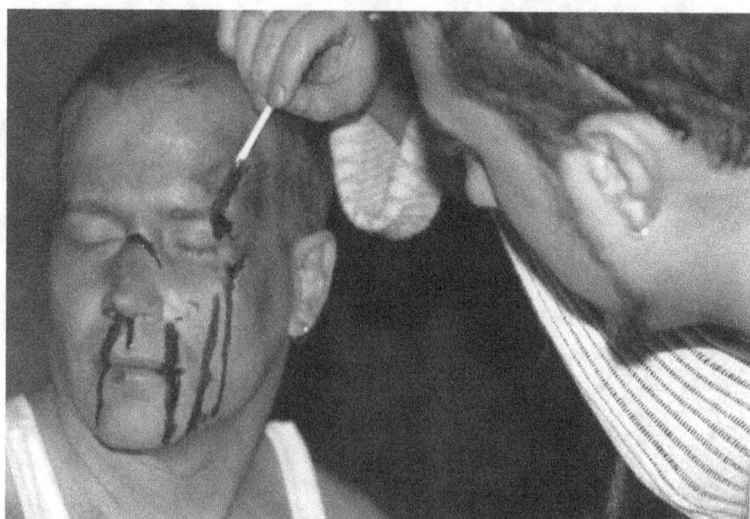
Ned getting makeup applied for the fight scene. When the makeup artist finished it really looked authentic, at this point it looks like makeup overkill.

One Sunday while setting up for the next scene, Sparrow's hands was tied, Lisa had on handcuffs, and Rob's hands were tied behind his back, they were reviewing their parts. The scene was a night shot that was being filmed on a bright sunny afternoon. The DP had a couple of the crewmembers to go outside and cover the window. Sorry to say, my neighbors were not happy; I was new to the neighborhood and within a few month of moving in the area I was shooting a movie. One neighbor in particular complained to the office, they simply said we know, and then asked, "didn't she tell you?"

I had handed out flyer and told everyone in the area that I was making a movie, I told them about the number of vehicles that would take up space. Have you ever had someone that was a nagging thorn in the side? The one neighbor, in spite of the office knowing, called the police. I live in the suburbs and in this neighborhood the police do not arrive with sirens blasting they come quietly. I was looking at the script and cueing the actors. The guys finished covering the window and had returned inside. They left the door standing slightly ajar. The police quietly drove up and walked in. Two of the hair and make-up artist was doing touch ups on the actors; three was in the kitchen eating. We simply did not hear them. The room suddenly became quiet; I stopped reading the script and saw the DP, crew, and actors had their hands up as though they were in a stick-up. In the middle of the room was an officer with a confused look on his face and his gun aimed at us. Standing on the steps looking down at the scene was a second officer chuckling.

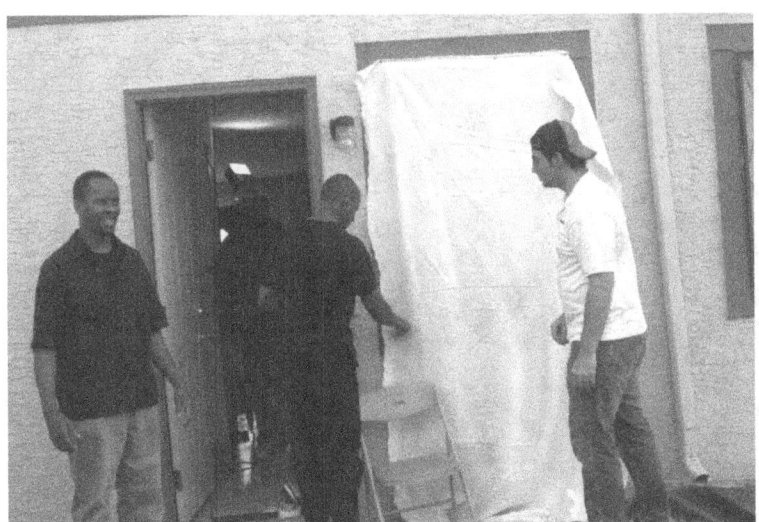
Ricky, Dennis, and Aaron covering the window.

Someone from the kitchen yelled, "Hey, the police is out side."

Ben, the set designer, and the DP showed the officer the weapons; it was interesting watching the officers movements, his hands handling the gun, his shoulders, his stance, his focus on the situation, while at the same time watch us. He gave the guns back to the set designer, and said, "Look like the real thing."

The officer's became calm, and noted the lights, cameras, mikes, props, actors in handcuffs and tied. The DP explained the reason for covering the windows, they understood. Before leaving, they told me to call the station everyday letting them know when and where we were filming. Both officers took one last look around the set and left smiling. It was priceless. We learned later that it was the swat team in the back of the apartment.

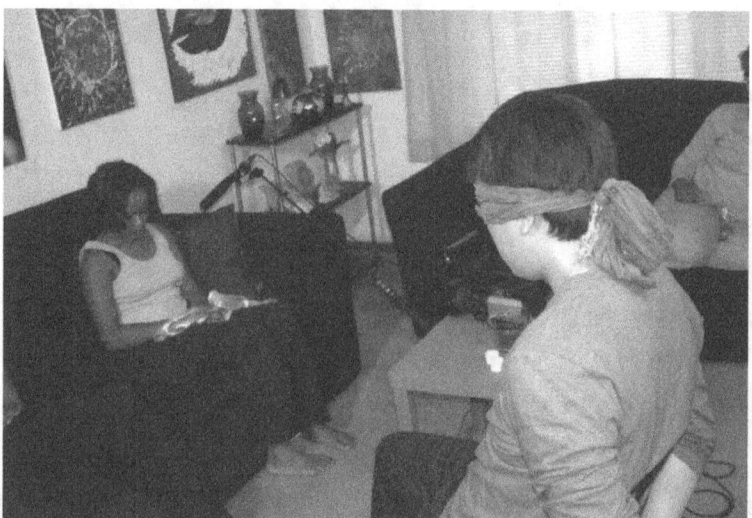

Hostages (Esther, David, Miesha) practicing their parts before police enters. Esther was a part of the kidnapping. David was her boyfriend and Miesha her roommate she pretended to be a hostage. Throughout the majority of the movie Miesha and David's eyes were covered so they could not identify the kidnappers.

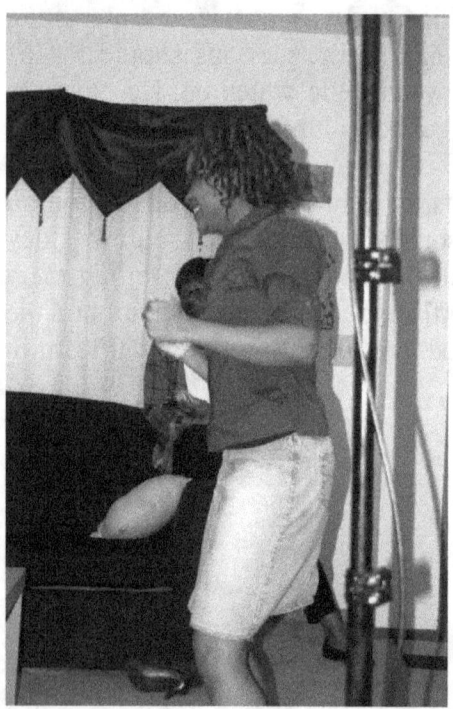

Esther is practicing the funky chicken for the dancing game. Sandra is in background.

Trust me, from that day forward I called the police reporting the day's activities. A few days later an officer stopped by to see the set, he said they were talking about us at the station. He was a gorgeous brother with a beautiful smile, oh my goodness. He handed me his card and said, "Call if you ever need anything," and then winked. I was seriously thinking about making the call until I saw a gold band on his finger. He suggested that I have and officer on set the next time we're filming. Actually, during pre-production I called the police department I ask for a police to be on set. Their salary at the time was $36.00 per hour. With a smile in my voice, I thanked him very much, and then I lied saying, "I will give you a call, sir."

I Hung up thinking, one day but not today.

On the eighth and last day, I had four scenes left to shoot, I chose the interrogation room we shot this scene on a weekday. Most of us had taken the day off, which turned out to be a good thing because we were on set for twelve hours. Though Ned was in this scene, he had returned to New York. We got creative before he left and recorded his voice blaming the other two kidnappers. While talking to the hostages in the interrogation room Detective Vince turned on the tape recorder and asked, "Does this sound like him?"

Each hostage recognized Zack's voice.

To shoot the remaining three scenes the same crew and actors, except Ned and the hair and makeup artist, returned the last week of October 2006. In all, it took eleven days to shoot the original screenplay.

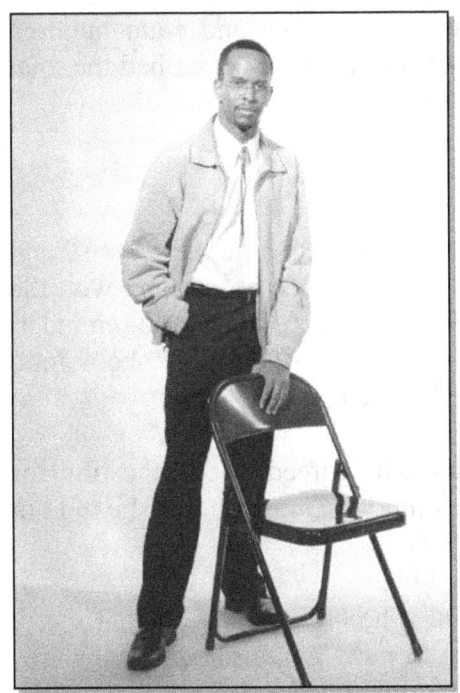

Ricky taking a promo shot as Detective Vince.

CHAPTER THREE

POST-PRODUCTION

The first DP was also an editor; he agreed to edit the film that was a relief, I did not have to hunt around for one. On the last day of filming in October, to confirm his position as the editor, he stood before Ricky, Dennis, and me declaring that he had to edit the film because of his unique shots. I knew trouble was boiling when he said that a producer he worked with no longer speaks to him. The list kept growing; he ended stating that another producer left his name out of the movie credits. He wanted someone to trust him; I thought why not, so I let him take the tapes hoping that my trust would not be obliterated. Regrettably, it was. He was supposed to email me scenes that he had worked on then call to discuss which ones I wanted to use, sadly I never heard from him. The second week of November, I called the two numbers he had given me; one was his mother the other his sister. The women had nothing good to say about him, nor did they know where he was.

One week before Christmas, he returned to Columbus without the tapes. He asked for three hundred dollars to purchase a hard drive, I gave him one hundred. February 2007, I received several DVD's that had two-thousand eight hundred hours of filming. All of the scenes coincided with the script; at least I had the total shots.

There was no one to blame but me.

In life, we make mistakes, we trust, we love, we learn, then continue forward and try not to repeat the same blunders. To control the recurrence of working with the same difficult people I bought a notebook to write their names down as a reminder. Over six years I only have seven names listed. Most people want to make a good film and they understand that the films out-come is based on their input.

A friend who lives here in Columbus is an editor; he agreed to edit the film for experience. He created two trailers; though it was fun working with him, he did not have the equipment to edit a complete movie.

I called a professor at Ohio University and asked if he knew of an editor. He did. March 2007, Ricky and I drove to Athens, Ohio to meet the third editor who was from Croatia. We hired him; he wanted five thousand dollars up front. I suggested that he complete the editing for two thousand and receive the remaining three when the movie comes out in theaters. He agreed.

When Rick and I returned to Columbus, we told Esther about the trip to Athens, she let me borrow the two thousand dollars. That evening the three of us drove back to Athens to give him the money and DVD's. He said that the University had just purchased a $42,000.00, finisher. With in two weeks he gave me a trailer and the DVD's, and then asked for three thousand dollars. I refreshed his memory and reminded him of the agreement that he had signed.

I called several times to see how he was coming along with the editing, he'd say, "pretty good."

The second week of May, he called in a panic saying that he must return to his country the first of June. He asked to be paid the three thousand dollars as soon as possible, after he receive the money he would complete the editing and help us enter the movie into a Croatian film festival. It all sounded good, but I paused to reflect back on our first meeting in March. I deduced if he could not accomplish the editing in three months, how would he finish in two weeks. I told him, no.

June 10, 2007, He called and asked if I wanted to purchase his hard drive for $450.00. He told me that all of the editing was on that piece of equipment. Enough was enough, at least I had the DVD's, I declined. I learned later that his visa had run out and immigration said he had to go, June 11 he was on his way home.

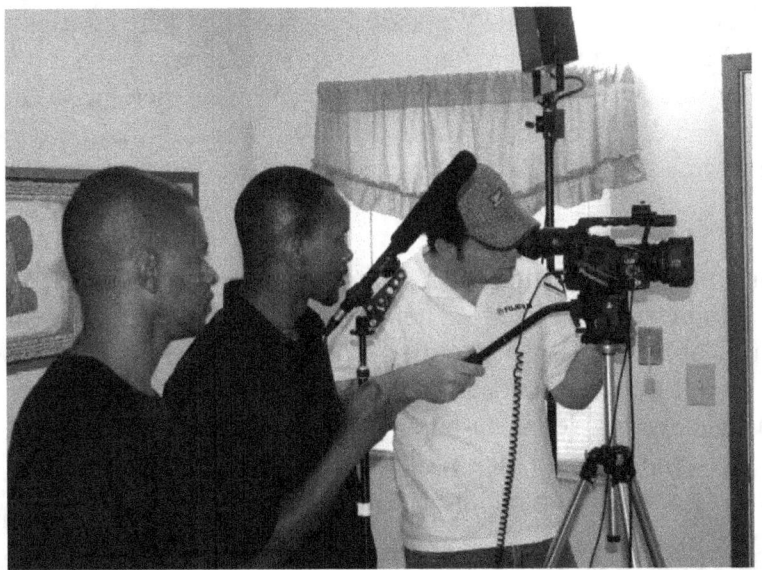

Dennis the gaffer, Ricky the sound man, and Aaron first camera operator.

The search continued for a fourth editor. I called the professor at Ohio University a second time; he quickly got me in contact with the fourth editor, who was working on his masters. Esther and I drove to Athens to meet him the second week of June. He showed us his work; he was talented but not as experienced as the third editor was. Beggars cannot be choosey, so I hired him. We discussed his charges. The memory of the first and third editors was too fresh in my mind; I had paid them upfront and still did not have a completed project, so I asked if he would accept a payment plan. He said yes, he was asking for seven hundred dollars. He said it would take him four months to finish the editing because he had schoolwork and his projects to edit. I said no problem. I paid him one hundred and seventy five dollars a month for four months.

After he finished editing the movie was fifty-minutes, it was too long for a short and too short for a feature film. Ricky and I went into writing mode. Between the summer and fall seasons of 2007, we went into preproduction and production. I asked four of the original actors to return, a host of new ones were hired, along with a new crew. There is a scene where Esther, David, and Laury, a new character and hit person, were outside talking. Ricky thought of the idea to take the camera up to the balcony and shoot the scene looking down at the actors. The shot was phenomenal.

One of the added scenes was Ricky lying on the police floor as Zack. This scene was shot in Esther's apartment; she was living in an historic renovated beautiful building that had all the original wood. The white French doors opened and lying on the floor was Ned dead from peanut oil. We shot the shoes and legs of Ricky because Ned is white and a few pounds heavier. After the last scene was shot we returned to my place for the wrap party. The majority of us experienced an oxymoron; we were happy and sad all at the same time. We were normal people who were a part of something out of the ordinary; sadly, we had to return to our lives statuesque

December 2007, the fourth editor graduated from Ohio University. The first week of February 2008, he completed the editing. Then stupid happened, he sent an email stating that he had lost his agreement and that I owned him seven thousand dollars. If I did not pay in full by a certain date I would not received the DVD's or the finished movie. To increase his demands he tried to jolt fright within me by saying he was hiring a lawyer and would take me to court. I found the agreement with his signature consenting to the seven hundred dollars.

Favor was on my side, in February the third editor returned to the US, his first stop was Ohio University. He had seen the finished work of the fourth editor. He called to say that the fourth editors work was amateurish but decent. I shared with him what he was trying to do. One week later, the fourth editor and his girlfriend delivered to my home the completed movie and all but one of the DVD's. I gave him the last payment.

April of 2008, in spite of its faults *The Blue Room* was booked in Hollywood Studio Theater for two weeks. I agreed with the theater to split the revenue down the middle. I did not have an issue with the agreement I was grateful for the opportunity. The actors had a chance to see themselves on a big screen, and the crew got to see their work.

At a restaurant, we had a Blue Room Movie Party for the stars, crew, and family members attended. Afterwards we went to the theater together to see the movie. A great number of people, who we did not know, was in the audience. After the film ended, we gathered in the foyer to talk. Strangers coming out of the theater room recognized the actors and went up to them to talk. It was so thrilling. The manager of Hollywood Studio Theater said, "people are coming to see your movie because of the marquee.
August of the same year I hired a fifth editor to add bloopers and outtakes to the DVD. By the end of 2008, it went on sale at amazon.com. I have no complaints, producing a film was an exciting journey despite the obstacles. I look back and see it all as lessons learned and hurdles that I overcame, and is going to do it again.

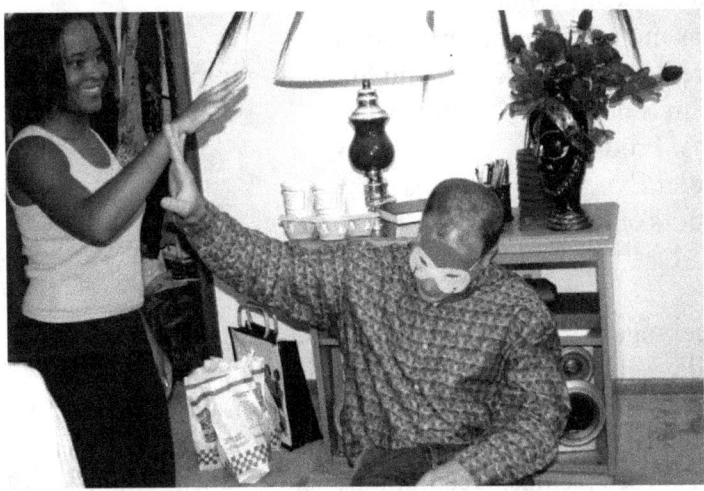

Esther and Ned playing around. When Ned entered the room with the hostages, he wore a mask so Miesha and David could not recognize him.

CHAPTER FOUR

HOW I PRODUCED A MOVIE WITH EIGHT THOUSAND DOLLARS

The budget below does not include pre-production. My phone service is with T-Mobile, with them I have unlimited calls and text, and a portion of my home was use as a office, no charge. I still have the receipts for food, water, and printing at Staples. Besides my office and phone, not included in the eight thousand dollars is the thirty-five dollar permit to shoot at the O'Shaughnessy Dam.

During production, we were a team of thirty crew and actors. Three for Post-production.

- $1,600.00   Meals Production
- $100.00   Meals Post Production
- $800.00   Gas money for crew and actors
- $2,000.00   Crew, cameras, Lights, and Sound Equipment
- $200.00   Film Stock
- $2,800.00   Post Production
- $400.00   Hotel Expenses - 2 rooms
- $100.00   Out takes

MEALS:
The scenes were shot weeknights from six to twelve midnight, and from 8 AM to 11 PM on Sundays. On Sunday, Esther and I prepared breakfast, and Lunch, grocery stores prepared the dinner meals. I found it to be cheaper than ordering from restaurants. To keep within the budget chewing gum, mints, health bars, sweets, chips, decorations, and medical supplies was bought at The Dollar Store.

- Grocery store Meals – chicken, cheese tray, relish tray, fruit tray, Pasta, garlic bread, and salads are cheap and stick to the ribs. Barbecued wings, pasta salad, and rolls is good, cheap, and filling.

Tuna salad, whole wheat bread, cheese, and fruit, on two of the days I ordered pizza, another evening Rally's.

To quench everyone's thirst, I got the juice, health drinks, and water from Aldi's.

GAS MONEY:
Everyone received $20 dollars. It did not fill their tanks; the money was simply a token of my appreciation.

FILMING EQUIPMENT:
I found a crew that owned their equipment – the equipment was inclusive in their pay.

FILM STOCK:
Was purchased at Myers a discount store here in the city.

EDITING:
Was done at Ohio University, I did not pay for their equipment, only the editors.

HOTEL:
Knights Inn, two rooms for thirty-two dollars a night, they gave me a huge deal since I was using the rooms for two weeks. Hair and makeup people was a crew of five, they were seniors from the Cleveland, Ohio Paul Mitchell School of Cosmetology, the school paid for their hotel rooms.

******

Before shooting a film to appear in the theater
- Any lawyer is able to set up a production company, however since the film industry is not set up like a typical business structure, it is to my understanding that it would be best to hire an entertainment lawyer. When I began Lavon Productions, LLC in 2000, the cost was $1800.00, I am sure the price has increased. I got lucky or blessed the lawyer that I found had moved from Paramount Pictures in Los Angeles, to Columbus, Ohio. He knew exactly what I needed to form a production company. The company will need, a city, county, and state business license, and an IRS Tax ID number. When I applied for a park permit, the clerk asked for my companies Tax ID.

- If money is in place, rent an office space. On the other hand, if funds are low a home office is perfectly satisfactory, the utilities and space may be claim on your taxes.

Story/Script
1. Pay for book rights – bargain the price or pay from the backend
2. Hire someone to write the script – bargain on the price or pay from the backend.
3. Write the script yourself – no out of pocket
    - Start with an idea; *The Blue Room* got its start based on Esther's blue wall.
    - What happed in that room? A kidnapping
    - Who was involved? Three executives, Chandler, Cole, Zack, two roommates, and a boyfriend.
    - What was the kidnapper's reason? Make money off rich relatives.
    - What was their motivation? 1. Chandler wife family was extremely rich. Greed. 2. Cole's wife rich uncle continues to abuse her; they are moving to another state to get away from her uncle. Protection. 3. Zack is clueless that Chandler hired him to take the blame. He thinks he's getting a big payoff. Decoy.
    - How to get the money? Kidnap selves for ransom.
    - Who was in charge? Sparrow with the help of a detective.
    - Sparrows reason. Save Chandler's wife from him, and to help Cole and his wife escape.
    - Where did the incident take place? In the safety of Sparrows home.

The audience should have an emotion for the characters, sadness, love, hate, joy, but never indifference. Have you ever seen a movie and sympathized with the bad guy? That's good writing.

- Money – hard and almost impossible to get, however, a few independent filmmakers have managed to acquire funding, still, too many of us have revolving doors with persistent no's. For that reason, I knew that I would not say no to me, or send myself a letter stating, "I do not accept unsolicited material", or "I am not interested at this time." So, I forged ahead went to the bank and used my money for the crew, actors, and equipment, Ricky helped to pay for the meals and Esther the editing.

Alternatively, borrow money from family members or friends, once the film is finished and booked in a theater take them out to dinner and pay for their theater ticket. Some of the biggest names in Hollywood funded their first movie. To name two, Vin Diesel earned money through telemarketing and Kevin Smith borrowed money from family and friends.

Pre-Production Schedule
Week one:
- Set a budget, find locations, finalize script, hire a director, producer, not unless you are the producer/director. If that is the case – hire an assistant director or unit production manager, production accountant to help manager the budget.

Week two:
- Began music clearance, which is very expensive. Find someone who writes music or use composers such as Beethoven, or Stravinsky the list is long. Fortunately, there is no charge to use the music. find someone that write music and is hankering to have his or her work published, began hiring the actors and crew.

Week Three:
- Permits – If an officer stops production, show him/her the permit. Shoot legal and not gorilla style. Design the set according to the theme of the script. Break the script down.

Week Four:
- Discuss wardrobe with the actors, have them to bring different outfit to the production office. If they do not have clothes to fit the character personality, get their size and purchase the clothes at a second hand store.

August 2012, I shot a short titled "If Only," in one of the scenes a character was going to be stabbed, I did not want to destroy his personal shirt so Esther and I went to a second hand store, they were selling brand new dress shirts for five dollars I bought two. That was a blessing. One of the shirts ended up with fake blood splattered all over it, the other he took home.

Later I thought that I should have kept the shirt for another short or film. I was happy, having fun, and not thinking.

Week Five:
- Transportation – how to get everyone from point A to point B, have the first production meeting and a reading with the actors even if there is not a full crew or cast, began with whose there. Schedule days actors need to be on set, complete film shoot schedule.

Week Six:
- Hair and Makeup - discuss the characters. Visit locations with the DP, light tech, and set designer.

Week Seven:
- Last reading or rehearsal, dress the set, hold last pre-production meetings.

Accommodate the list according to your needs.

Production – follow the film shoot schedule, things like weather, accidents, illnesses cannot be controlled, but over shooting a scene should be prohibited. Otherwise, it will detain and lengthen days of filming, remember actors and crew have other projects.

Post production – Telling the story.

******

Getting the film booked in the Theater:

AMC and Regal guidelines are very different, still, neither of the theaters accepts pornography and they will not book a film without a rating.

Contact Motion Picture Association of America (MPAA) to have the film rated. Visit their website at http://www.mpaa.org/, their contact information is listed on their site. They are incredibly patient, knowledgeable, help with filling out their long detailed forms, answer questions, and discuss cost, which is a small percentage of the budget.

After the process with MPAA has begun; contact AMC and Regal to get their guidelines. Both theaters have smaller rooms for independent films. If the film does well they will transfer it to a larger room.

The question the two theaters will ask, "What is your advertising budget? What is the genre of the film?" AMC headquarters is located in Kansas

City, MO. Regal Entertainment Group is in Knoxville, TN. Give them a call.

I did not have an advertising budget, so I called local theaters and asked for their booking procedures. As expected I received several, "no's", or they would consider the film if a noted star was attached. Finally, a definite yes, "The Blue Room" was booked in a theater for two weeks.

If you have not shot a short or film and have the desire to do so, just do it even if all you have is fifty dollars.

The script should be written in courier new, font size eleven or twelve. The format of scripts has changed several times, last year twice. However, Esther Luttrell has written several books on script writing she stays up-to-date on Hollywood changes. Visit her website at http://www.estherluttrell.com/. For a small fee, she will help you get the script formatted correctly and aid in the building of the characters. She assisted me with the last script that I wrote, based on Ricky's third book titled, *Repeat Offender*. Through emails and phone calls for eleven months we worked together and she trained me. I now have a perfect script. She will do the same for you. Look her up.

Lastly, if AMC or Regal will not show the film, ask local theaters, if they say no. I had a friend who paid a local theater four hundred dollars to run his movie. If that is not possible, have a showing at home, buy some popcorn, chips, and candy charge everyone a small fee or have them to bring something to eat.

Through it all, love what you do and have fun doing it.

CHAPTER FIVE

The Blue Room Screenplay

TITLE OVER

DAY OF INCIDENT

1. INT. APARTMENT SPARROW BEDROOM DAY

It is 6:30 A.M. Sunday morning.

SAPARROW JENKINS (Black) and LISA BENNETT (White) are roommates. Their apartment is full of various artworks by Sparrow. The apartment décor is youthful. Sparrow and Lisa are in their twenties. They are in their nightclothes

Sparrow wakes up, sees THREE MEN standing over her bed, one of the men grabs Sparrow and covers her mouth. Another man grabs ROBERT LEE (Asian); Sparrow's boyfriend, lets out a shallow yell, as he struggles with his assailant.

2. INT. APARTMENT LISA BEDROOM DAY

Lisa is in her bedroom when she hears commotion coming from Sparrow's room. She dials the phone.

CHANDLER VILDERMANN, one of the assailants, enters her room. He covers her mouth and speaks into the phone.

                    911 OPERATOR
    9-1-1.

                    CHANDLER
        Sorry ma'am, I was dialing 4-1-1.

Chandler hangs up and drags Lisa out of her bedroom downstairs where Sparrow and Robert are tied and have a blindfold over their eyes.

3. INT. APARTMENT LIVING ROOM DAY

In the living room COLE HARRIS, another assailant, ties and put a blindfold on Lisa.

Cole looks down and sees that Robert is trying to get lose.

> COLE
> Have those handcuffs? This one is getting lose.

Chandler pulls from his pocket a pair of handcuffs.

Chandler (White) is in his thirties. He is an aristocrat by way of his wife whose family are billionaires. Chandler is loud, abrasive, but kind.
Cole (Black) is one of the business mangers at Chandler's company. Cole and Chandler are friends. Cole is soft spoken and very business like.

ZACK HUNT (White) is the third assailant. He's a computer operator at Chandler's company. Zack has nervous energy, he's a liar who drinks too much coffee, which makes him edgy.

> CHANDLER
> Sorry to inconvenience the three of you we need
> a place to hide out for the next twenty-four hours.

CREDITS ROLL

4. INT. APARTMENT LIVING ROOM DAY

The three hostages squirm in their chairs.

> ZACK
> (loudly)
> Sit still, or...

Chandler talking to Zack.

> CHANDLER
> That's not necessary.

Cole tries to calm them.

> COLE
> This will be over before you know it.

Chandler to Cole.

> CHANDLER
> If you where in their place would you...

Zack detest Chandler, Chandler feels the same towards Zack. Zack yells at Chandler.

                    ZACK
              (loud and rough)
    What makes you all knowing? Who made you god?

                    COLE
        This is a hideout. Lower your voice.

Zack gives Cole an evil look. Looking at Zack, Cole's eyes softens. He feels sorry for the man, because according to Zack, his wife is a monster of a woman.

                    COLE
              Please.

Looking at Zack

                    CHANDLER
              Watch them.

Chandler looks over at Cole.

                    CHANDLER
              Follow me.

Chandler walks toward the back door. Cole follows Chandler. Zack is agitated.

                    ZACK
              What about me?

                    CHANDLER
              Watch them.

5. EXT. APARTMENT BACKYARD DAY

Chandler and Cole in the backyard, Chandler looks back and sees Zack pacing and watching them and not the hostages.

6. INT. – EXT. APARTMENT LIVING ROOM - BACKYARD DAY

Zack POV –

Zack watching Chandler and Cole, Cole turns around and sees Zack.

7. EXT. APARTMENT BACKYARD MORNING

Cole and Chandler talking. Cole sneezes.

> CHANDLER
> Think we can trust him, Cole?

> COLE
> Doubt it.

8. EXT. – INT. APARTMENT BACKYARD - LIVING ROOM DAY

Cole and Chandler see Robert trying to get up even though he's tied to the chair and has a blind fold on. Zack violently push Robert.

> CHANDLER (VO)
> Right now, we need Zack.

> COLE (VO)
> Need him? Chandler, he's a nervous mess.

9. EXT. APARTMENT BACKYARD DAY

Chandler and Cole talking.

> CHANDLER
> Until we get what we want,
> Zack is a part of the team.

10. EXT. – INT. APARTMENT BACKYARD - LIVING ROOM MORNING

Chandler and Cole POV – Zack looking at them.

11. INT. APARTMENT SPARROW BEDROOM NIGHT

TITLE OVER:

> NIGHT BEFORE THE DAY OF INCIDENT

Sparrow and her boyfriend Robert are talking.

Sparrow appearance and actions are professional. She is soft-spoken and very likable. Robert is an engineer. He is in love with Sparrow.

While lying in bed Sparrow shares a memory.

> ROBERT
> Sweet dreams Sparrow.

Robert reaches for the lights but Sparrow stops him.

                    SPARROW
Robert wait. Did I ever tell you about my parents?

                    ROBERT
No.

                    SPARROW
My father killed my mother.

                    ROBERT
Sparrow, if you don't want to tell me,
don't make up a lie.

                    SPARROW
I'm not. He beat my mother and me, put my
mom in the hospital where she died. And where
he's a doctor.

                    ROBERT
For real?

                    SPARROW
Yeah.

                    ROBERT
You're not abusive.

                    SPARROW
Prayer changes people. Anyway, I was eighteen
when mom whispered that she hid some money at
home. On her dying bed she told me to go home,
get the money, and buy a ticket under a
different name. Go to America.

                    ROBERT
You're not an American?

                    SPARROW
Robert listen. After she told me what to do,
mother died. I kissed her on the forehead.
Took her picture. Left. At home I found false
ID's for the both of us. We were to escape after
I graduated from high school. I had three months

to graduation.

ROBERT
You got a MBA, right?

SPARROW
Before leaving, I wrote a letter to the police. My first stop was Miami. I used Mom's ID to purchase a car. Bought a map, closed my eyes and pointed. My finger was on Ohio.

ROBERT
How much money did she save?

SPARROW
In Cleveland, I met a friend, he showed me his birth certificate. Stuck it in my purse, went to an office store, made a copy. Bought identical paper as the birth certificate. Took it back to my friend and slipped it between the cushions of the couch.

ROBERT
Why?

SPARROW
He was looking for it he didn't know I had it. I drove to Columbus, got on the computer and made me a birth certificate. Born in the USA. When I turned nineteen, I got my GED, then on to college.

ROBERT
Where's your father?

SPARROW
Don't know.

ROBERT
You've lived in this country for six years. Sometimes it takes a few generations for a family from another country to completely lose their native accent. You sound authentic.

SPARROW
I watched a lot of TV, went to movies, hung

around Americans. Lost most of my Jamaican accent within a month.

                ROBERT

But your father...

                SPARROW

I walk on eggshells. If he finds me, he'll kill me.

                ROBERT

You told the police, maybe he's in jail.

                SPARROW

Maybe, is not definite.

                ROBERT

How much money...

                SPARROW

Fifteen thousand dollars.

Robert turns the lights out and then on.

                ROBERT

That much in a money jar?

                SPARROW

No, a briefcase, locked in her suitcase, with a pile of clothes stacked on top.

                ROBERT

Wow.

Robert turns the lights off.

                ROBERT

Why tell me now?

                SPARROW

I don't know. Strange feeling.

TITLE OVER

            DAY AFTER INCIDENT

12. INT. INTERROGATION ROOM DAY

Robert is with DETECTIVE VINCE in an interrogation room where the officer is probing to find out what happened.

There is a small tape recorder on the table so no information is lost.

> DETECTIVE VINCE
> You didn't know that she wasn't an American?

> ROBERT
> No.

> DETECTIVE VINCE
> All this time, no clues?

> ROBERT
> Wait until you hear her talk. She has no accent.

> DETECTIVE VINCE
> And her family?

> ROBERT
> Didn't know that either. Her father was abusive.

> DETECTIVE VINCE
> She kept a lot from you.

> ROBERT
> He killed his wife. For her to go through that...I...I can't believe she raised herself. Got her MBA.

> DETECTIVE VINCE
> Sounds strong.

> ROBERT
> She is. During our hostage situation she was brave.

Robert looks at the detective tie.

> ROBERT
> Like your tie.

> DETECTIVE VINCE
> Thanks. It's a bolo.

> ROBERT
> You're from Texas?

> DETECTIVE VINCE
> No. Like the style. You mentioned money.

> ROBERT
> Yeah, from her mother. She did a lot of good with the money. Very smart, cunning. Knows how to get things done.

> DETECTIVE VINCE
> Cunning? Sounds like she kept a lot from you?

> ROBERT
> What are you saying Detective Vince?

> DETECTIVE VINCE
> Robert I'm here to find answers to the incident at your apartment.

> ROBERT
> Sparrow and Lisa's apartment.

> DETECTIVE VINCE
> Any assistance will be helpful.
> Did you try to escape?

13. INT. APARTMENT LIVING ROOM DAY

Sparrow, Robert, and Lisa are tied up and have their eyes covered. Zack is pacing nervously in front of them. Robert is fidgeting the most between the hostages.

Zack and Cole are watching the hostages.

> ZACK
> Why are you fidgeting?

Zack push Robert to make him stop squirming.

> ZACK
> Stop it. You make me nervous.

> SPARROW
> No need for that. He's good.

ZACK
You watch your mouth Sp...girl.

LISA
We're all going to die, I know it. They're not going to let us go.

ZACK
Calm down sweet thing. This will be over soon.

LISA
Please don't kill me!

ZACK
I said calm down!

Robert hands are hand cuffed behind his back. Robert attempts to escape, Zack reaches for him. Robert pulls out of Zack's grasp. Zack and Robert fall on the floor.

Robert, tries to slide his body through his arms. Zack grabs him, pulls Robert in a standing position and slams him on the couch.

ZACK
What do you think you're doing?

Zack slams Robert into his seat. Chandler enters the room.

CHANDLER
What's going on?

ROBERT
I had to use the bathroom, he...

ZACK
He was escaping!

Chandler to Robert

CHANDLER
I don't want to hurt you.

SPARROW
Please don't, we won't try anything else.

ZACK

I don't believe her.

                CHANDLER
Shut up! This will be over shortly. There's no reason for an escape, or for anyone to be afraid.

                LISA
We're going to die, I know it.

                SPARROW
Lisa calm down, we'll get through this.

                COLE
Listen to your friend.

                CHANDLER
Twenty-four hours, that's all we need. When we get what we came for, your lives will return to normal.

                ZACK
I say we make an example of this one.

Zack puts his hands around Robert's neck.

                CHANDLER
No need for that.
    (To Cole)
Watch them.
    (To Zack)
Come here.

14. INT. APARTMENT KITCHEN DAY

Chandler and Zack in the kitchen, while Cole watches over the hostages.

                CHANDLER
You couldn't watch three people for five minutes?

                ZACK
They distracted me. I'm nervous. Need coffee. Cole was doing nothing.

                CHANDLER
From what I see, you don't. Calm down.

> Think and breathe. The next phase of this
> plan is soon, we need you to be ready.
> Are you ready?

                        ZACK

I'll think of my wife.
              (takes a sip of
              coffee)
Yea, I'm ready.

                    CHANDLER

I know. I feel the same way about mine.
That's why we're doing this.

                       ZACK

Sorry. I'm calm.

                    CHANDLER

Lets get back in there. Keep them comfortable
and quiet.

15. INT. APARTMENT LIVING ROOM DAY

Chandler and Zack returns to the living room. Cole stands guard as the hostages fidget.

                       COLE

Everything cool?

                       ZACK

Yea.

                       LISA

Why us? My parents aren't that rich, really it's a
muse. We don't have that much. The media...

                    CHANDLER

Lisa shut up.

                       COLE

Thank you. She talks to much.

                    CHANDLER

Like I said before. No one will be harmed, you
will come out of this unscathed.

                        ZACK
            Un what?

SOUND FX: Phone rings.

Cole feels his pocket and answers the phone.

                        COLE
            Hello honey...

                        LISA
            Help! Help we've been...

Chandler covers her mouth with his hand.

                        CHANDLER
            Quiet he can't hear.

                        COLE
            Everything is okay. Call you later.

                        CHANDLER
            Put the phone on vibrate.

                        COLE
            Sorry about that.

Chandler to Lisa

                        CHANDLER
            As for you, you're talking privileges are over.

Chandler to Cole

                        CHANDLER
            Give me something to gag her with.

Cole hands him a scarf and pulls out two others for the other hostages.

                        CHANDLER
            Thanks. Would you two like the same treatment.

                        SPARROW and ROBERT
            No.

16. INT. INTERROGATION ROOM DAY

Robert is with Detective Vince telling the story.

>DETECTIVE VINCE
>He had enough scarves for everyone?

>ROBERT
>I guess. Scarves, rags, handkerchiefs what difference does it make.

>DETECTIVE VINCE
>You don't live there.

>ROBERT
>No I spend the night sometimes, Lisa would disagree.

TITLE OVER:

>DAY BEFORE THE INCIDENT

17. INT. APARTMENT LIVING ROOM DAY

Sparrow is drawing on a pad while Lisa is reading. Robert is in the bathroom.

>LISA
>I don't see why he has to be here all the time.

>SPARROW
>Lisa, must we go through this every time he's here.

>LISA
>No Sparrow, that would mean every single day.

>SPARROW
>Robert is not here that often. You're jealous.

>LISA
>No I'm not. I have everything I want.

>SPARROW
>I know. Your parents are lawyers.

>LISA
>Why you say it like that. I here a negative tone.

SPARROW
No tone.

LISA
Yes tone. I can't help it if my parents are successful. Where are your parents? Who do they work for?

SPARROW
My parents don't defend the guilty. And make the innocent suffer.

LISA
That is not true. People are innocent until proven guilty. You know that. Everyone knows that. Don't understand why people down my parents. They are good...

SPARROW
You need a man.

LISA
I'm independent thank you, and do not need any man to help me. I'm fine by myself.

SPARROW
You haven't had a boyfriend since freshman year in college. That was many years ago. What are you waiting for.

LISA
The perfect man. Unlike some.

SPARROW
Robert is fine, don't hate, because you don't have anyone to love you.

Robert walks into the living room from the bathroom fanning his hand.

ROBERT
Don't want to go in there, whew.

LISA
You always stinking up stuff.

ROBERT
Contamination is more like it, ha-ha.

LISA
Honestly, Sparrow why do you put up with him?

Robert goes into the kitchen.

LISA
I know you're not going to eat up all of our food. Why do you let him eat up everything.

SPARROW
Robert paid for half the groceries, I paid for the other, he can do what he want.

LISA
You always get what you want. Boyfriend can come over whenever. You hang up all your art work. Why blue paintings, they're depressing.

SPARROW
You could look at it that way. Possibilities are endless. It reminds me of home. Blue is peaceful. The sky is blue, the ocean is blue...

LISA
Hmph. Cleveland, big deal. Lake Erie, more like dirty green.

SPARROW
This is my Blue Room.

LISA
(whisper under her breath)
Freaks room, more like it. What about Michael Angelo...

Sparrow begins to hum as she continues to draw. She ignores Lisa.

LISA
I know you hear me. Fine. Keep on singing to yourself, but you know I'm right. Robert is over here to much.

Robert enters the Living room with a snack in his hand. He sits next to Sparrow.

> ROBERT
> Want some baby.

> SPARROW
> Sure.

Sparrow looks up and sees Lisa going up the steps.

> SPARROW
> Lisa, you moved in with me, remember?

> LISA
> You won't let me forget it.

> SPARROW
> Like you remind me of your fortune.

18. INT. INTERROGATION ROOM DAY

Robert and Detective Vince in the room.

> ROBERT
> They always argue. Can't believe they're friends.

> DETECTIVE VINCE
> Defense attorney's?

> ROBERT
> Yeah I think she want to be a lawyer.

> DETECTIVE VINCE
> She would know how to get people free?

> ROBERT
> I guess.

> DETECTIVE VINCE
> That's her parent's job. People do a crime. They save them from doing the time.

> ROBERT
> You don't like defense

attorneys?

>   DETECTIVE VINCE
> We're on opposite sides of lady justice.

>   ROBERT
> Did you study psychology?

>   DETECTIVE VINCE
> Took a few courses. There where three kidnappers, three hostages. But I talked to a fourth about an hour ago. When did he come into play?

19. INT. APARTMENT – LIVING ROOM - DAY

Cole is sitting in front of the three hostages; he puts the phone in his pocket.

>   COLE
> Who wants to hear a knock-knock joke?

>   SPARROW
> I don't, I am thirsty.

>   COLE
> Don't like jokes.

>   SPARROW
> Water, please.

>   ROBERT
> Its ok Sparrow. We'll be fine.

>   COLE
> Listen to your man.

>   SPARROW
> Water.

>   COLE
> One water coming up.

Cole goes into the kitchen.

>   ROBERT
> Sparrow what are you doing?

                    SPARROW
Leaving, I feel pent up.

                    COLE (OS)
Robert are you thirsty? Can't have you dying of dehydration.

                    SPARROW
          (whisper)
Say yes.

                    ROBERT
Yea.

                    COLE (OS)
Tomorrow all this will be behind you.

                    SPARROW
     I'm out.

                    ROBERT
Sparrow no. The other two are gone and will be back any minute.

                    SPARROW
All the more reason for me to leave.

Sparrow gets up and stumbles her way to the door.

Cole sees this and runs from the kitchen to the living room.

                    COLE
     Where you going?

                    ROBERT
Sparrow sit down.

                    SPARROW
I will not be a hostage.

                    COLE
You're making this hard on yourself.

Cole and Sparrow tussle a little when Chandler walks in with Zack who is wearing a mask.

Zack is staggering like he's drunk.

Sparrow runs into Chandler, which knocks her down. Cole grabs her.

> CHANDLER
> What's going on?

> COLE
> She's trying to escape.

> CHANDLER
> She is, take her upstairs.

> ROBERT
> No wait, she's nervous.

> CHANDLER
> Rough her up a little.

> ROBERT
> That's not necessary.

> COLE
> Come with me.

> ROBERT
> No wait.

Cole grabs Sparrow and forces her upstairs.

> ROBERT
> Please don't hurt her.

> SPARROW
> Please don't hurt me.

> CHANDLER
> Teach her a lesson for trying to escape.

> ROBERT
> Take me.

> CHANDLER
> Shut up!

Chandler kicks Robert then checks the handcuffs.

Chandler knocks Zack on the couch. He falls on Lisa.

                              LISA
                    (mumbling)
                  Get off me.

                            ROBERT
                What are you doing?

                          CHANDLER
                We've added another person to the mix. He is the key to us getting what we want, and you getting your life back.

We hear sounds of Sparrow yelling and smacks.

                         SPARROW (OS)
                I'm sorry.

                          COLE (OS)
                When I say sit, sit.

Robert tries to get up but Chandler pushes him down.

                          CHANDLER
                Sit down! She's fine for now.
                No more trying to escape.

SOUND FX: KNOCK AT THE DOOR

                          CHANDLER
                Don't anyone move.

Chandler answers the door.

                          CHANDLER
                Good to see you.

                            ROBERT
                Who's there.

                          CHANDLER
                As you can see, we had to blindfold them.

> Don't want them to see the mastermind behind this. A girl is upstairs with Cole. Go up and give instructions.

20. INT. INTERROGATION ROOM DAY

Detective Vince is more into what Robert is saying.

> DETECTIVE VINCE
> Could you describe this woman.

> ROBERT
> Not really. I was wearing a blindfolds. I could smell her perfume.

> DETECTIVE VINCE
> Another kidnapper came in.

> ROBERT
> Yes. Do you have pop?

> DETECTIVE VINCE
> What?

> ROBERT
> I need something to drink. I feel like I am having a panic attack. I can't breathe. If they had hurt Sparrow...

> DETECTIVE VINCE
> Robert its ok. Take deep breaths.

Detective Vince slides a pad and pen in front of Robert.

> DETECTIVE VINCE
> I'll get you a pop.

> ROBERT
> Thank you Detective Vince.

21. INT. APARTMENT LIVING ROOM DAY

Zack and Chandler are in the kitchen while Cole watches the hostages.

> COLE

Sorry to bother you.

                    LISA

I bet you're not really sorry. You all are just the same. Come in, take what you want, do as you please. What do you want? What have we done? I don't Understand.

                    COLE

I understand your hostility.

                    LISA

I doubt that. My parents are powerful people and you will pay. Hear me. You will pay.

                    COLE

I am not a violent man, but you keep pushing...

                  SPARROW

Lisa, keep quiet.

                    LISA

Me. You should be worried about them not me. They came in the middle of the night, dragging us out of bed. Making demands and holding us hostage. They're the ones...

                    COLE

Enough.

Zack and Chandler walks back into the room.

                    COLE

I'm tired of her talking.

Chandler pulls out the handkerchief and gags Lisa.

                CHANDLER

When are you going to learn?

22. INT. INTERROGATION ROOM DAY

Detective Vince talks with Lisa.

Lisa is nervous, fidgety; she swings her hair back and forth. She thinks a lot of herself. She acts like a beauty queen, she's obnoxious.

Detective Vince is not impressed with her.

>   DETECTIVE VINCE
>   From the very beginning.
>
>   LISA
>   I assumed that Rob told you what happened.
>
>   DETECTIVE VINCE
>   I want to hear your version.
>
>   LISA
>   Wouldn't call it a version. Just what happened,
>   you know. Version implies, false, story, a tale,
>   something made up. I'm going to tell you the
>   truth.
>
>   DETECTIVE VINCE
>   Any day now.
>
>   LISA
>   I was in bed when a sound came from Sparrow's
>   room. Normally when Robert spends the night
>   they are quiet. But this time there was a strange
>   noise.
>
>   DETECTIVE VINCE
>   Did you call the police?
>
>   LISA
>   Yes, but a man came into my room.
>
>   DETECTIVE VINCE
>   Is this the man.

Detective slides a photo in front of Lisa.

>   LISA
>   It was too dark. My eyes were covered.

Lisa toss her hair out of her face. She fidgets, straightens her clothes. Basically do things to get the Detective's attention

He's not amused.

> DETECTIVE VINCE
> Continue.

> LISA
> I never heard a noise. Isn't a break-in loud? Glass breaking, doors being knocked down, anything. There was no noise.

> DETECTIVE VINCE
> You were asleep.

> LISA
> I should have heard something. I was scared, I still should have heard something.

> DETECTIVE VINCE
> You said they blindfolded you?

> LISA
> Yes and tied my hands. Then he dragged me to the living room, threw me in a chair next to Sparrow and Robert.

> DETECTIVE VINCE
> After they tied and blindfolded you, then what happened?

> LISA
> One of them got a call. I yelled for help. They gagged me. Don't know why Robert and Sparrow didn't chime in.

> DETECTIVE VINCE
> Who knows?

23. INT. APARTMENT LIVING ROOM DAY

The hostages are on the couch, tied and blindfold. Lisa is the only one gagged.

The three kidnappers are in the room.

Zack is sipping on coffee.

> **ZACK**
> Good coffee. Calms my nerves.

> **CHANDLER**
> Like I was saying. We don't want your money.
> (To Lisa)
> I know your parents have a lot of money, but its not nearly enough.

> **SPARROW**
> Why us?

> **CHANDLER**
> Your place is perfect. Its in the woods.

> **SPARROW**
> You're sick.

> **CHANDLER**
> Good people do questionable things all the time, when pushed.

> **SPARROW**
> I don't hear Lisa talking. I assume you put a plug in her mouth.

> **COLE**
> Had to.

Chandler nods at Cole.

> **CHANDLER**
> Watch them.

> **COLE**
> Okay.

Chandler and Zack leave the apartment.

There is silence for a moment as Cole sits in front of the hostages looking at them.

> **ROBERT**
> (whisper)
> Sparrow, I think we're alone.

COLE
No I'm still here.

LISA
(muffled)
I'm thirsty.

COLE
I'll get the water. Keep quiet.

Cole removes the scarf.

LISA
There's spring water in the fridge. Two ice cubes please.

COLE
This isn't a restaurant.

LISA
I'm hungry.

COLE
Tell me about yourselves.

ROBERT
What?

COLE
We can sit here in silence...

ROBERT
I'm not telling you about me.

COLE
I know a couple of knock-knock jokes.

SPARROW
Please don't.

COLE
I'll tell you about my wife. Many years ago, I saw

her in class. I knew she was my soul mate.

                ROBERT
That's what Sparrow is to me.

                SPARROW
Thanks baby.

                LISA
Somebody call the police I am being killed over here...

                SPARROW
She has no one.

                LISA
Do you fail to realize that we are hostages in our home. This is not the time to play nice with this man. He's not a co-worker.

                SPARROW
Uh...could you...

                COLE
On it.

Cole gags Lisa.

Obviously Lisa is complaining.

                COLE
My wife family is a problem. They've tried to break us up.

                SPARROW
Is everything ok with you?

                COLE
With us yes. Her Uncle...

Cole begins to tear up a little bit.

                COLE
Is abusive. When someone you love is being abused, you suffer with them.

> SPARROW
> I know.

> COLE
> But I feel defenseless. That tears me up. I'm doing what I can to make her life better.

> ROBERT
> This isn't helping her.

Cole's cell phone vibrate, he answers.

> COLE
> You are. Ok. I'm ready.

Cole hangs the phone up.

> COLE
> Let the games begin.

24. INT. INTERROGATION ROOM DAY

Detective Vince talking with Lisa.

> DETECTIVE VINCE
> Is that when they brought the fourth hostage in?

> LISA
> Yea.

Lisa struggles to talk; her mouth is dry and she pulls out of her purse a compact and lipstick.

> DETECTIVE VINCE.
> Ms. Bennett, wait until after...

> LISA
> I'm thirsty.

> DETECTIVE VINCE
> Coffee, tea, pop...

                    LISA
            Water will do. Spring water if you have any in
            a place like this. Two ice cubes. Don't fill
            the glass.

Detective Vince gets her a glass of water.

He sets the glass of water in front of her and walks out.

25. INT. OUTSIDE INTERROGATION ROOM DAY

Detective Vince walks over to DETECTIVE 1.

                    DETECTIVE VINCE
            She irks me.

                    DETECTIVE 1
            Why?

                    DETECTIVE VINCE
            Something about her is fake.

Detective Vince walks away.

                    DETECTIVE VINCE
            Get on my nerves when people try to be something
            they're not.

26. INT. INTERROGATION ROOM DAY

Detective Vince enters the room
                    LISA
            Do you have bottled water?

                    DETECTIVE VINCE
            Continue.

Lisa takes a sip.

                    LISA
            They brought the new guy in. Took Sparrow to her
            bedroom. Put Robert and me in my bedroom.

                    DETECTIVE VINCE
            Why?

                          LISA
            They where wearing a mask, took our blindfolds
            off and shoved us into my room.

27. INT. APARTMENT LISA'S BEDROOM DAY

Chandler push them into Lisa's room. Chandler is wearing a mask.

                        CHANDLER
            I'll be right back. Don't go anywhere.

Chandler leaves the room.

Robert and Lisa is not wearing blindfolds and their hands are not tied.

                          ROBERT
            I'm nervous.

Chandler returns with some fast food.

He is wearing a mask.

                        CHANDLER
            Your computer is disconnected. We took the wires.

Chandler sets the food on the desk.

                        CHANDLER
            Here's lunch.

He hands them the food.

                        CHANDLER
            Don't try anything, you do, Sparrow and that man
            out there will be the only two hostages seeing
            tomorrow's sunrise.

Chandler leaves.

Both begin eating their food.

Robert picks at his food.

                          ROBERT

> My appetite is gone. These people are holding us hostages. Why are they so friendly? It's Confusing.

Lisa is gulping down her food.

> LISA
> I don't know. Eat.

> ROBERT
> I can't get out of my mind what Sparrow told me last night.

> LISA
> What was that?

> ROBERT
> It was personal.

28. INT. INTERROGATION ROOM DAY

Lisa is sipping on her water.

> LISA
> No spring water?

> DETECTIVE VINCE
> None. Continue.

> LISA
> They brought in Sparrow which made Robert happy. Things got really interesting when they brought in the masked guy.

29. INT. APARTMENT LISA'S BEDROOM DAY

Sparrow is eating her food and having a conversation with Robert and Lisa.

> SPARROW
> Hmm. That's true.

SOUND FX: A LOUD BANG AT THE DOOR

Chandler is knocking hard.

This startles everyone in the room.

>   ROBERT
> I think we can take them.

>   SPARROW
> No, no. Lets do what he says. I don't want to get hurt again.

>   LISA
> This is crazy Robert is right. We can definitely...

>   SPARROW
> They said you're next, Lisa.

Chandler and Cole push the masked hostage into the room.

>   SPARROW
> They're gone.

>   LISA
> I hate this. Locked up in my own room.

>   SPARROW
> I wonder who's he?

>   ROBERT
> Hey Mister take off your mask.

Sparrow kneels down and is about to remove the mask when Zack moves and makes a noise.

This startles everyone.

The new hostage gets up and looks around the room.

>   ZACK
> Where am I?

>   SPARROW
> You've been kidnapped.

>   LISA
> Are you okay?

                    ZACK
Did you say kidnapped?

Zack looks at everyone.

                    ZACK
Are you the kidnappers?

                    SPARROW
No. We didn't have anything to do with the
kidnapping.

                    LISA
It's a little hard to understand you, take the
mask off.

                    ZACK
No, no. The less you know about me...

                    ROBERT
You're one of us.

                    LISA
Who are you? You must be important.
More important then me, anyway.
                    SPARROW
What's your name?

                    ZACK
My head hurts.

                    ROBERT
Your voice sounds familiar. Have we met?

                    ZACK
Uhh...My wife is behind all of this.

                    LISA
Ouch. Talk about trouble in paradise.
My mother and father would never do something
like this to one another.

                    SPARROW
Lisa this isn't about you.

> ROBERT
> A woman came in wearing a lot of perfume.

> ZACK
> That was my wife.

> SPARROW
> That's some wife you have.

> ZACK
> Yea. She's the only one who would do this.

Robert looks over at Sparrow.

> SPARROW
> I would never do that.

> ZACK
> That's what I thought. Until today.

Zack coughs.

> LISA
> Maybe you should take the mask off.

> ROBERT
> Its cool, we're not with them.

> ZACK
> I'm fine.

> ROBERT
> I can barely understand you.

> ZACK
> I'm fine.

Lisa and Robert reaches for the mask, Zack pushes their hands away.

30. INT. INTERROGATION ROOM DAY

Lisa sips a little from her cup and talks to Detective Vince.

> LISA
> Sparrow pulled the mask off.

> DETECTIVE VINCE

>   I thought you said you and Robert did.

>   LISA
>   We tried, he fought us off.

>   DETECTIVE VINCE
>   I see. He looked like this?

Detective Vince slides a picture over to Lisa. We cannot see the picture but Lisa looks down at the photograph.

>   LISA
>   That's him.

Lisa slides it back to Detective Vince.

>   LISA
>   I can't imagine being held hostage by a family member.

>   DETECTIVE VINCE
>   Most crimes in America are committed by family members.

>   LISA
>   Not in my family.

>   DETECTIVE VINCE
>   What happened next?

>   LISA
>   They dragged Bob out.

>   DETECTIVE VINCE
>   Bob?

>   LISA
>   That's what Robert called him. He never gave his real name. I think they mentioned it on TV, can't remember.

>   DETECTIVE VINCE
>   I see. Continue.

>   LISA

Then Sparrow was taken to her bedroom, I think, and Robert had to leave. The guy explained it, but I wasn't paying much attention.

                        DETECTIVE VINCE

You was alone?

31. INT. APARTMENT LIVING ROOM NIGHT

Lisa is on the couch, tied up, gagged, and blindfolded.

Cole is sitting across from her.

                                  COLE

           Its going to be over soon.

Lisa tries to respond.

                                  COLE

    Sorry.

Cole removes the scarf from her mouth.

                                  LISA

Good.

                                  COLE

You said your parents are lawyers.

                                  LISA

    Need one?

                                  COLE

All is not as it seems.

                                  LISA

Right.

                                  COLE

Like I said before. No one is going to die. We won't gain from that. The only thing we'll get is locked behind bars.

                                  LISA

Then let me go.

                              COLE
            I looked your parents up, they are country lawyers,
            working out of a raggedy building. With a clientele
            of less than twenty.

                              LISA
            My parents are honorable. They work for mankind.

                              COLE
            You mean they work to free the bad guy.

                              LISA
            So? You're a bad guy.

                              COLE
            No, I am one of the good guys.

                              LISA
            How can that be?

                              COLE
            Its true that two wrongs don't make a right.
            Sometimes you have to undo one wrong by any
            means. That's why we're not here to harm you,
            hold you against your will, yes. Bring harm, no.

                              LISA
            Is Sparrow okay?

                              COLE
            She's fine, trust me.

Cole checks his pocket. His phone is vibrating.

                              COLE
            Hello. They're on the way to get it now. He's
            not there is he? Good. I'm telling you after
            tonight, you won't have to worry anymore.
            See you soon.

Cole put his phone back in his pocket.

                              LISA
            Wife?

                        COLE
            Yes.

Chandler and Robert enter the apartment. Chandler is holding a manila envelope Robert is carrying two briefcases.

                        CHANDLER
            We got it.

32. INT. INTERROGATION ROOM DAY

Lisa has changed from perky to depressed.

                        DETECTIVE VINCE
            He returns, what happened then?

                        LISA
            I can't continue right now.

                        DETECTIVE VINCE
            You ok?

                        LISA
            I've never been in love. That's depressing. I can't
            go on. A couple of kidnappers bragging about
            being in love, and I've never experienced it.
            That's not fair. My life is depressing.

                        DETECTIVE VINCE
            Need some time Ms. Bennett?

Detective Vince gets up to leave.

33. INT. OUTSIDE INTERROGATION ROOM DAY

Detective Vince is stretching in front of the interrogation room trying to relax his muscles.

He shakes the tension off, and drinks from a bottle of spring water.

Detective 1 walks over to him.

                        DETECTIVE VINCE
            Bring Robert in.

34. INT. APARTMENT LISA'S BEDROOM DAY

Lisa and Robert are eating their lunch.

        LISA
  Think we'll get out of this.

        ROBERT
  Yea. At least I hope so.

SOUND FX: A LOUD BANG ON THE DOOR
Sparrow is shoved into the room. Chandler is wearing a mask.

        SPARROW
  Not so hard.

        CHANDLER
  Get in there.

Chandler slams the door.

Robert rush over to Sparrow.

        ROBERT
  You okay? I was worried.

        SPARROW
  Yea, I'm fine.

        LISA
  I thought they killed you.

        ROBERT
  They didn't touch you, did they?

        SPARROW
  No, no they didn't do anything like that. I heard a
  female voice.

        LISA
  We heard her also.

        ROBERT
  I smelt her perfume.

        SPARROW
  There's another guy in the living room. Who is he?

> LISA
> He's our ticket out of this mess.

Sparrow eats her food.

> SPARROW
> We should concentrate on what we're going to do.

> LISA
> I'm scared. What if they get their money and kill us anyway?

> SPARROW
> Have you seen there faces?

> LISA
> No.

> SPARROW
> Then you're fine. As long as we can't see who they are then we can't pick them out of a lineup.

> ROBERT
> We know their voice. We're half way there.

> SPARROW
> Hmm. That's true.

SOUND FX: A LOUD BANG AT THE DOOR

Chandler opens the door. The hostages jump.

Chandler enters.

35. INT. INTERROGATION ROOM DAY

Detective Vince is very interested in Robert's story.

Robert has a piece of paper with random notes scribbled on it.

> DETECTIVE VINCE
> Did you say you could recognize the kidnapper's voice.

ROBERT
Yes.

Detective Vince stands up.

DETECTIVE VINCE
I'll be right back.

Detective Vince leaves the room.
Robert sips on some soda and writes a few notes down.

Detective Vince returns and puts a new tape in the recorder.

DETECTIVE VINCE
Call it a hunch.

The Detective plays the tape.

ZACK
(from the tape
recorder)
I was at home, and they wrestled me out of bed. I tried fighting back, they where too strong.

DETECTIVE VINCE
(from the tape recorder)
What happened next?

ZACK
(from the tape recorder)
I was in this strange apartment surrounded by three people.

Detective Vince turns the tape player off.

Robert leans into the tape player.

ROBERT
That was him.

Detective Vince slides a picture in front of Robert.

DETECTIVE VINCE
You recognize this man?

Robert looks at the picture.

>   ROBERT
> Yea, that's Bob. At least that's what I called him. He didn't give his real name and I can't remember what the media said it was.

>   DETECTIVE VINCE
> I'll be right back.

Detective Vince grabs the picture and heads out the room.

36. INT. OUTSIDE OF INTERROGATION ROOM DAY

Detective Vince finds Detective 1 near the room.

>   DETECTIVE VINCE
> Go pick him up.

Detective Vince hands Detective 1 the photo.

37. INT. INTERROGATION ROOM DAY

Detective Vince returns in the room.

>   DETECTIVE VINCE
> Thanks Mr. Lee.

>   ROBERT
> But it doesn't make since.

>   DETECTIVE VINCE
> That's why I'm here. What happened Next?

38. INT. APARTMENT LISA BEDROOM DAY

Zack is pushing Lisa and Robert away from him.

Sparrow reaches up and snatches the mask off his head.

>   SPARROW
> There now, feel better?

Zack stares at Sparrow for a moment shocked that she grabbed the mask.

>   ROBERT

>   You okay?

Zack snaps out of it and focus on the hostages.

>   ZACK
>   Yea. I'm better now.
>   ROBERT
>   My name is Robert. That's Sparrow my girlfriend,
>   and Lisa, Sparrow's roommate. What's your name?
>
>   ZACK
>   You don't need to know.
>
>   ROBERT
>   I'll call you Bob for now.
>
>   ZACK
>   My wife hired someone to kidnap me, and rough
>   me up.
>
>   LISA
>   Did you hear a noise?
>
>   ZACK
>   A what?
>
>   LISA
>   Noise. A loud bang at your window, or door or
>   something.
>
>
>   ZACK
>   No I can't say that I did.
>
>   LISA
>   Neither did I.
>
>   SPARROW
>   We sleep upstairs, with our door closed.
>   Plus, we were up late, playing the dancing game.

39. INT. INTERROGATION ROOM DAY

Detective Vince is confused.

>   DETECTIVE VINCE

>   Name that dance?

>   ROBERT
>   Yea.

40. INT. APARTMENT LIVING ROOM NIGHT

Sparrow is cuddled by Robert while Lisa is on the loveseat.

>   ROBERT
>   Good choice of movie Sparrow.

Robert turns the television off.

>   ROBERT
>   Just when you think they could not squeeze another
>   pint of blood in the film, WHAM!!! Another head...

>   LISA
>   I can't go to sleep.

>   SPARROW
>   What's the matter Lisa.

Robert and Sparrow laugh and head upstairs.

>   LISA
>   Stay down here with me for a moment.

>   ROBERT
>   C'mon Lisa you'll be fine.

>   LISA
>   I'm serious. You have each other, I have no one
>   but sheets, four walls and a vivid imagination
>   of blood and guts.

Sparrow and Robert sits down on the couch.

>   SPARROW
>   What do you want to do?

Lisa thinks for a moment, she gets up and starts dancing the Twist.

                    ROBERT
          You alright?

                    LISA
          I'm fine, guess what dance this is?

Sparrow and Robert are confused they stand up to leave.

                    SPARROW
          Goodnight Lisa.

                    LISA
          I'm serious. Sit down, guess.

They sit.

Sparrow looks at her watch.

                    SPARROW
          Its late.

Lisa dance the twist.

                    ROBERT
          The twist. That's easy.

                    LISA
          Okay, now it's your turn.

                    SPARROW
          What?

                    LISA
          Whoever guess the dance, its their turn. It's a
          game my family play.

Robert and Lisa trade spots and Robert dance the salsa.

                    SPARROW
          That's easy, salsa.

Sparrow takes Robert's place.

Sparrow starts doing the funky chicken, Robert and Lisa are laughing.

                    SPARROW

> Come on you guys, stop laughing and guess.

ROBERT
It's – it's – I don't know.

LISA
Lost me on that one roomy.

SPARROW
The funky chicken.

41. INT. APARTMENT SPARROW'S BEDROOM NIGHT

Sparrow and Robert are in bed.

Sparrow is fidgeting with her phone.

ROBERT
I really like that game.

SPARROW
Didn't know that Lisa and her family had fun.

They laugh.

ROBERT
That was some movie. Can you imagine being held hostage. What a nightmare.

SPARROW
No I can't.

ROBERT
Who are you calling this late at Night?

SPARROW
Setting the alarm.

She sets the phone down.

SPARROW
Robert do you love me?

ROBERT
Yes. You okay?

                    SPARROW
         I'm fine.

                    ROBERT
         Sweet dreams Sparrow.

Robert reaches for the lights but Sparrow stops him.

                    SPARROW
         Robert wait. Did I ever tell you about my parents?

42. INT. INTERROGATION ROOM DAY

Robert dance in his chair.

                    ROBERT
         It was a fun game.

                    DETECTIVE VINCE
         I see. Lets get back to Zack.

43. INT. APARTMENT LISA BEDROOM SUNSET

SOUND FX: LOUD BANGING AT THE DOOR

This startles everybody in the room. Chandler is not wearing a mask.

Chandler yells through the door.

                    CHANDLER (OS)
         Put your blindfolds on.

                    LISA
         I'm tired of this.

                    SPARROW
              (yells at Chandler)
         Why? Put your mask on.

Chandler sticks his gun through a small opening of the door.

Everyone puts their blindfolds on. Zack puts his mask back on.

                    SPARROW
         Blindfolds on?

                    ROBERT, LISA, ZACK
    (unison)
Yea.

                          SPARROW
We're ready.

Chandler walks into the room with Cole. Cole and Chandler immediately begin tying their hands behind their backs.

                          CHANDLER
Glad to see everyone cooperating. We're taking a road trip.

                            LISA
I knew they where going to kill us.

                          CHANDLER
Shut up!

                            LISA
We're going to end up dead in a cornfield.

                          CHANDLER
Keep talking, I'll gag you.

                            COLE
She talks too much.

                          CHANDLER
I agree. I'm not taking her, she'll drive me crazy.
    (pointing to Zack)
I can't take him because its to dangerous to move him.

                            COLE
He's bad luck.

Chandler pauses for a moment. He looks at Sparrow and Robert.

                          CHANDLER
Bad luck?

                            COLE

>   Yeah, you have to keep your luck positive when
>   you're doing things like this. I read it in a book.

>   CHANDLER
>   You read it in a...never mind. So its either him or
>   his pretty little girlfriend.

Chandler and Cole looks at one another and then at Sparrow.

>   CHANDLER and COLE
>   Girlfriend.

>   SPARROW
>   I won't go.

>   ROBERT
>   Take me instead.

Chandler holds the gun while Cole finish tying Robert's hands.

>   CHANDLER
>   Don't do anything stupid.

Cole pushes Robert toward Chandler who is near the doorway.

>   CHANDLER
>   We're going downstairs.

Chandler looks at Zack.

>   CHANDLER
>   Stay here. The rest of you downstairs.

Cole pushes Lisa toward Chandler.

>   SPARROW
>   I'm not going anywhere.

Cole reaches for Sparrow.

Sparrow removes her blindfold and grabs Cole's gun.

Chandler immediately grabs Robert and holds the gun to his head.

>   ROBERT
>   What's going on, what's happening?

                    SPARROW
Let him go.

                    CHANDLER
Taking your blindfold off was a stupid move.

                    ROBERT
Sparrow no.

Chandler presses his gun into Robert's head.

                    CHANDLER
Drop the gun.

                    SPARROW
You drop your gun.

                    CHANDLER
I can get another partner, how long will it take you to find someone like Rob.

                    ROBERT
Sparrow listen to the man.

                    SPARROW
No.

                    CHANDLER
By the count of four Robbie's brains will be splattered all over this room.

                    LISA
Sparrow for crying out loud, drop the gun!

                    CHANDLER
One.

                    ROBERT
Remember when you asked if I loved you?

                    CHANDLER
Two. Might I remind you that all I need is the masked man.

                    ROBERT

If you love me, put the gun down.

Chandler cocks the gun.

                        CHANDLER
Three.

                        SPARROW
Alright.

Sparrow tosses the gun on the bed.

Chandler releases Robert, he keeps the gun pointed at the hostages.

                        CHANDLER
Your girlfriend was smart. Go downstairs.

44. INT. APARTMENT LIVING ROOM NIGHT

Robert and Lisa are tied to the chairs.

Chandler is sitting in front of them.

We hear faint sounds of Sparrow getting smacked around.

                        CHANDLER
That was stupid of your girlfriend to play hero.

                        ROBERT
I'll be glad when this is over.

                        CHANDLER
I told you, follow the rules.

                        ROBERT
Are you going to tell me your life story.

                        CHANDLER
You and I are going for a ride.

                        ROBERT
I'll do whatever you want.

Chandler looks over at Lisa.

                        CHANDLER

You're unusually quiet.

Lisa says nothing.

Cole comes running downstairs.

                    COLE
She's taken care of.

                  ROBERT
What did you do? Is she okay.

                CHANDLER
She's fine.

                    COLE
Uh...finish talking to the masked man's wife she's going to make the call. Our guy is watching Sparrow and the masked man.

                CHANDLER
Good. Watch her.

45. INT. INTERROGATION ROOM DAY

Robert and Detective Vince are still talking.

              DETECTIVE VINCE
You said they mention his name.

                  ROBERT
Not them, the TV reporter.

46. INT. APARTMENT LIVING ROOM NIGHT

Cole walks into the kitchen while Chandler turns the TV on.

A NEWS REPORTER is on the set talking about the kidnapping.

            NEWS REPORTER (OS)
Police has no lead on the possible kidnapping of Zack Hunt who was taken earlier today from his home. There is no info on his wife's whereabouts, or who committed this crime. This is...

Chandler turns the television off.

> COLE
> Is this good luck or bad luck?

> CHANDLER
> Good.

Chandler unties Robert's hands and feet.

Chandler and Robert leave the apartment.

47 INT. CAR NIGHT

Parked in the alley, Chandler and Robert wait in the car.

Chandler is wearing a ski mask; he unties Robert's hands.

> CHANDLER
> Remove your blindfold.

Robert removes his blindfold, but keeps his eyes close.

Chandler places the briefcase in Robert's lap.

> CHANDLER
> Open your eyes.

> ROBERT
> I don't want to see your face.

> CHANDLER
> I'm wearing a mask, open your eyes.

Robert looks over at Chandler and sees the ski mask and gun. Chandler points to the trashcans.

> CHANDLER
> Remember what I told you?

> ROBERT
> Yes. I'm suppose to take this briefcase, switch it with the one in the trashcan.

> CHANDLER
> Switch?

                    ROBERT
          Take this briefcase and place it exactly in the
          same spot.

                    CHANDLER
          Correct.

                    ROBERT
          What if the police are watching?

                    CHANDLER
          They are.

Robert gets out of the car.

                    CHANDLER
          If you make one move...

Chandler holds his phone up.

                    ROBERT
          I know, Sparrow gets it.

                    CHANDLER
          You're a smart man.

48. EXT. STREET NIGHT
The van pulls up in front of the trashcan.

Robert runs over makes the switch, runs back to the car.

Both vehicles pull off.

49. INT. CAR NIGHT

Robert enters the car with the briefcase. Chandler ties Robert's hands and blindfolds him.

                    CHANDLER
          Two more stops and we're home free.

Chandler removes his mask.

50. INT. APARTMENT LIVING ROOM NIGHT

Chandler and Robert enter into the apartment with the briefcases and manila envelope.

                    CHANDLER
        We got it!

Cole takes Robert to the couch.

                    COLE
        I knew you could do it.

                    CHANDLER
        Was there any doubt.

                    ROBERT
        Now what?

                    CHANDLER
        We wait.

51. INT. INTERROGATION ROOM DAY

Detective Vince is with Robert in the room. He realizes how they where able to pull the switch off.

                    DETECTIVE VINCE
        So, that's how they did it.

                    ROBERT
        What was in the case?

                    DETECTIVE VINCE
        A note.

52. EXT. STREET NIGHT

Detective Vince and Detective 1 stands by the trashcan after the vehicles leaves.

                    DETECTIVE VINCE
        They didn't take the money, strange.

Detective Vince opens the briefcase.

He pulls out a piece of paper.

53. INT. INTERROGATION ROOM DAY

Detective Vince and Robert in the interrogation room. Robert finished his soda.

>   ROBERT
> What did it say.

>   DETECTIVE VINCE
> It lead us to Mr. Hunt.

FLASHBACK

54. EXT. ABANDON PLAYGROUND DAY

Zack is tied to an abandon swing set.

Detective Vince and Detective 1 finds him.

Detective Vince removes the mask.

Zack has bruises on his face.

>   DETECTIVE VINCE
> I'm the Detective on this case.

>   ZACK
> Man am I glad to see you guys.

>   DETECTIVE VINCE
> We're taking you in for questioning.

55. INT. INTERROGATION ROOM DAY

While Detective Vince and Robert are talking, Detective 1 enters the room and whispers in Detective Vince's ear.

>   DETECTIVE VINCE
> Oh, okay, put Ms. Jenkins in room three.

Detective 1 leaves the room.

>   DETECTIVE VINCE
> Thank you Mr. Lee.

Detective Vince stands up.

Robert follows his lead and stands up as well.

>   DETECTIVE VINCE

> Follow the Detective.

56. EXT. PARK DAY

TITLE OVER:

> MONTHS EARLIER

Chandler and Cole are dressed in business casual.

They're outside their office building near some trees and benches.

> COLE
> I love nature.

Cole sneezes.

> COLE
> Nature don't love me.

> CHANDLER
> Me too. That's why I had this park added.

> COLE
> The plan have to work. It's my way of protecting my wife.

> CHANDLER
> After this, you can start over again.

> COLE
> What about you?

> CHANDLER
> It's taken care of.

> COLE
> You're asking for fifty mill. Are you worth that?

> CHANDLER
> Yes, because of me their company is a billion dollar corporation.

Sparrow runs up to the men.

> **SPARROW**
> Sorry, for being late. Had to get the expense report out.

> **CHANDLER**
> No problem. You got the key?

> **SPARROW**
> Yes.

Sparrow hands Chandler the key.

> **SPARROW**
> I'll leave my purse on the couch, once inside, drop it in there.

Zack suddenly walks up on them.

> **ZACK**
> You're planning something, I want in. If you say no, I will call the cops.

> **COLE**
> Who are you?

> **CHANDLER**
> Zack...right?

> **ZACK**
> Cole knows who I am, you're Chandler Vildermann, the owner of this company. You're his little assistant, Sparrow.

> **COLE**
> How do you know what we're planning.

> **ZACK**
> I've been following you these past few weeks. I know you're up to something and I want in. I want to get revenge on my adulterous wife.

> **CHANDLER**
> With him the plan will work.

                    SPARROW
          (whisper)
          You sure?

                    CHANDLER
          (whisper)
          Trust me.

57. INT. OUTSIDE OF INTERROGATION ROOM DAY

Detective Vince is visibly upset. He walks up to Detective 1.

                    DETECTIVE VINCE
          They're taking Zack to the hospital. Follow the
          ambulance and make sure it gets to the hospital.
          Something smells fishy.

58. INT. INTERROGATION ROOM DAY

Sparrow sits alone in the room until Detective Vince enters and reacts to her beauty.

                    DETECTIVE VINCE
          Miss Jenkins...

                    SPARROW
          Call me Sparrow.

                    DETECTIVE VINCE
          Sparrow, I am Detective Vince, I have a few
          questions regarding the night of the incident.

                    SPARROW
          I heard that you caught them.

                    DETECTIVE VINCE
          Tell me what happened.

                    SPARROW
          I was asleep, some men dragged me downstairs,
          tied my hands, put blindfold on my eyes.

Sparrow shows Detective Vince her scars around her wrist.

                    SPARROW
          See what they did to my wrist.

                    DETECTIVE VINCE
          Have any idea how they got in?

                         SPARROW
                    No.

59. INT. APARTMENT SPARROW'S BEDROOM NIGHT

Sparrow and Robert are asleep. Sparrow's phone vibrates.

Sparrow slowly gets up so she won't wake Robert.

                         SPARROW
                    (whisper)
               Going to the bathroom.

60. INT. APARTMENT LIVING ROOM NIGHT
Sparrow answers the door.

Chandler, Cole, and Zack enter. They whisper.

                         SPARROW
               Why didn't you use the key?

                         CHANDLER
                    It didn't work.

                         SPARROW
               Let me see the key.

Sparrow takes the key.

                         SPARROW
               Oops. This is the key to Robert's place.

                         ZACK
               Oops. This isn't funny.

                         CHANDLER
                    (shout whisper)
               Lower your voice Zack.

Sparrow goes upstairs. We hear her flush the toilet.

                         COLE
               What if her roommate wakes up?

CHANDLER
She won't.

61. INT. INTERROGATION ROOM DAY

Detective Vince is making notes.

SPARROW
I was trying to get lose and escape but the rope was to tight.

DETECTIVE VINCE
Did you ever get loose?

SPARROW
Almost.

62. INT. APARTMENT LIVING ROOM DAY

Lisa and Robert are tied in chairs with blindfolds on Sparrow isn't.

Cole is putting the cell phone away.

Cole points to his watch, then outside.

COLE
(mouth)
They're outside, you ready.

Sparrow nods her head.

COLE
Who wants to hear a knock-knock joke?

SPARROW
I want a glass of water.

COLE
Don't like jokes.

Cole gets up from his chair and walks into the kitchen.

SPARROW

I'm out.

ROBERT
Sparrow no. The other two are gone and will be back any minute.

SPARROW
All the more reason for me to leave.

Sparrow gets up moves around on the couch as if she's having a hard time.

Cole sees her and walk into the living room.

COLE
Where you going?

ROBERT
Sparrow sit down.

SPARROW
I'm leaving.

COLE
Stop making this hard on yourself.

Cole runs into the living room, he pretends to attack Sparrow.

Chandler walks into the apartment with Zack. Zack is holding a mask in his hand.

CHANDLER
What's going on?

COLE
She's trying to escape.

CHANDLER
Take her upstairs.

Chandler looks over at Zack who has on the mask.

ROBERT
No wait, she's fine. She's ok.

CHANDLER
Rough her up.

Chandler flash three fingers in Zack's face.

> ZACK
> Three birds are flying away.

> COLE
> (talking to Sparrow)
> Come with me.

> SPARROW
> Please don't hurt me.

> CHANDLER
> Teach her a lesson.

63. INT. APARTMENT SPARROW BEDROOM DAY

Sparrow is upstairs with Cole in her bedroom.

Cole takes out a rope and wraps it around Sparrow's arm.

> SPARROW
> This is going to hurt isn't it.

> COLE
> A little we have to make it realfor the police.

> SPARROW
> I know.

> COLE
> Make sure to scream.

Cole jerks the rope tight so it burns her wrists.

> SPARROW
> Ahhhh!!! Is that good.

> COLE
> That was believable.

Cole takes the rope off.

> SPARROW

> It hurts.

> COLE
> Your boyfriend is probably panicking. The rope left a pretty good mark.

> SPARROW
> Now for the phone calls. Got the pre-paid phone.

> COLE
> Yes.

> SPARROW
> Good, no record.

64. INT. APARTMENT LIVING ROOM DAY

Chandler stands by the door and pulls out a bottle of perfume.

Zack is sitting on the loveseat playing with the mask.

Chandler knocks hard at the door.

SOUND FX: KNOCK AT THE DOOR

> CHANDLER
> Don't anyone move. I have a gun

Chandler opens the door and shuts it. No one enters.

Chandler opens the bottle of perfume and waves it in the air.

> CHANDLER
> Good to see you.

> ROBERT
> Who's there?

> CHANDLER
> As you can see, we had to blindfold them.
> Can't have them looking at the mastermind
> behind the plan. You can go up, make the phone calls.

Chandler points to Zack and then to the two hostages.

> CHANDLER

> (mouth)
> Watch them.

Zack nods his head.

65. INT. APARTMENT SPARROW'S BEDROOM DAY

Sparrow is on the phone, the mouthpiece is covered with a cloth.

Chandler enters the room.

> SPARROW
> Get the money now or your son-in law will be killed. No cops, no agents. I'll call back with details.

Sparrow hangs up.

> CHANDLER
> How's it going?

> SPARROW
> First two calls complete, one left.

> CHANDLER
> I have to go downstairs, before Zack does something foolish.

> COLE
> Still getting hamburgers?

> CHANDLER
> Yes, Cole you get lunch.

> SPARROW
> Robert and Lisa eating?

> CHANDLER
> Yes.

Chandler and Cole leaves the room.

Sparrow dials the phone.

66. INT. APARTMENT HALLWAY DAY

POV Top of stairs:
We see Zack standing in front of the door at the bottom of the stairs talking on his phone.

                ZACK
Chandler thinks he's in charge. What he don't know I'm in charge. He told me and not the others that he's asking his dad for over two million dollars. Baby we're going to be rich.

67. EXT. PARK OUTSIDE OF OFFICE DAY

Chandler, Cole, Sparrow, and Zack talking about their plans.

                CHANDLER
This might work.

                SPARROW
   (whisper)
You sure?

                CHANDLER
   (whisper)
Trust me.

                ZACK
Why are you doing this?

                COLE
My wife's Uncle rapes her once or twice a week. She hides out at a friend's house until I get home.

                CHANDLER
Call the police?

                COLE
I do, over and over.

                CHANDLER
Does she have relatives?

                COLE
Her mom, she's in a nursing home.

Cole sneezes.

                    ZACK
Bless you. I have allergies. Peanuts.

                    CHANDLER
Those can be deadly.

                    ZACK
You're right.

                    CHANDLER
Interesting. You were talking about your mother-in-law.

                    COLE
She was in a car accident, left her brain dead.

                    ZACK
What does this have to do with anything.

                    COLE
Everything. The other day my wife couldn't get in contact with any of her friends, she went to the police station and parked. An officer came out and told her to move the car or she would be towed. She told them about her uncle. He told her to move on She went home, her Uncle was inside our home. I've had enough. He's destroying my wife's life.

                    CHANDLER
Does he have money?

                    COLE
His company made five hundred thousand last month.

68. INT. INTERROGATION ROOM – DAY

Detective Vince and Sparrow.

                    SPARROW
The masked man's wife made calls. I don't know what she talked about, they took me into another room.

                    DETECTIVE VINCE

>   Anything else?

>   SPARROW
>   When she came in she said something about getting
>   cash for her husband.

>   DETECTIVE VINCE
>   What happened next?

>   SPARROW
>   They brought the masked man into the room.

69. INT. APARTMENT SPARROW'S BEDROOM NIGHT

Sparrow is in her bedroom waiting for Chandler to enter.

She picks up a picture of herself and Robert.

>   SPARROW
>   (talking to the picture)
>   I hope one day I can explain why I did this baby.

She kisses the picture. Chandler enters the room with food.

>   CHANDLER
>   Time to eat.

>   SPARROW
>   Good. I'm starving.

>   CHANDLER
>   Don't eat now, wait until we throw you into
>   Lisa's room.

>   SPARROW
>   Think I should tell Robert.

>   CHANDLER
>   No. Better to leave him in the dark. You inherit
>   or found or got some money from a lost relative.

>   SPARROW
>   I'll figure it out.

>   CHANDLER
>   Don't tell Lisa?

                    SPARROW
          I'm not.

                    CHANDLER
          She brags about her parents money.

                    SPARROW
          They don't have much.

                    CHANDLER
          If my wife and I dropped down to their salary I
          would hang myself. I'm not being pompous
          Sparrow. What a person has or make is for that
          person and their family to know. Some people
          might think I'm rich and powerful. To a
          Billionaire he might think I have a good job.

Chandler looks at his watch.

                    CHANDLER
          Its game time. Remember when you get in, your
          first goal is to remove Zack's mask.

70. INT. APARTMENT HALLWAY DAY

Sparrow has her blindfolds on and the bag of food in her hands.

Chandler bangs on the door.

Sparrow is shoved into the room.

                    SPARROW
          Not so hard.

                    CHANDLER
          Get in there.

He slams the door.

71. INT. APARTMENT KITCHEN DAY

Cole and Zack are eating.

Chandler joins them.

CHANDLER
Ready Zack.

ZACK
Yes, but I've been thinking. Maybe my cut should be a little higher.

CHANDLER
What?

ZACK
I'm the one taking all the risks. I have to be in there with them dressed up as some hostage, the cops are going to interrogate me.

COLE
They will ask you questions. You're a hostage the police wouldn't interrogate you.

ZACK
I should get more money. You're getting a big bundle from your dad.

COLE
Dad!?

ZACK
He's getting two million.

Cole looks confused.

ZACK
Between the four of us, I'm taking the biggest risk.

CHANDLER
Let me inform you its my plan and ideas that are getting us here. Sparrow is risking the most.
She has to act like a hostage in her home amongst her friends. All you have to do is don a
Halloween mask and act like you've been beaten.

ZACK
If I don't get more money. I will squeal like a pig.

CHANDLER
Is that right.

Chandler grabs the back of Zack's head and slams his face onto the table.

Chandler then shoves his gun into Zack's face.

                    ZACK
         What are you doing? It's not loaded.

                 CHANDLER
         Try me.

                    COLE
         Whoa, Chandler we don't need this.

                 CHANDLER
         Its alright Cole. As far as you're concern, you are
         a hostage wearing a Halloween mask provided by
         your wife. Is that clear?

                    ZACK
         That's clear.

                 CHANDLER
         Good. If I'm unclear tomorrow's headline will read,
         kidnapping gone bad when Zack Hunt held as
         an hostage was killed. He is survived by, you fill
         in the blank.

Chandler releases his grip and sits down. He eats.

                 CHANDLER
         Finish your food.

72. INT. APARTMENT OUTSIDE OF SPARROW'S BEDROOM DAY

Chandler and Cole are with Zack who has the mask over his head.

                 CHANDLER
         Ready?

                    ZACK
         Yea.

Chandler knocks hard at the door.

                    CHANDLER
            We're coming in. Put your blindfolds on, or reap
            the consequences.

73. INT. APARTMENT LISA BEDROOM DAY

Everyone in the room looks startled.

                    ROBERT
            I think we can take them.

                    SPARROW
            No, no. Lets do what he says. I don't want to get
            hurt again.

                    LISA
            This is crazy Robert is right. We can definitely...

                    SPARROW
            Put your blindfolds on.

Lisa and Robert puts there's on. Sparrow only acts like she has her on and then pulls it down.

                    SPARROW
            We got them on.

Zack walks into the room and plops down on the floor.

                    SPARROW
            They're gone.

Sparrow acts as though she's pulling off her blindfolds with Lisa and Robert.

                    LISA
            I hate this. Locked up in my own room.

                    SPARROW
            I wonder who is he?

74. INT. INTERROGATION ROOM DAY

Detective Vince snaps Sparrow out of her dream like daze.

>   DETECTIVE VINCE
> You okay Sparrow?
>
>   SPARROW
> Yes I'm fine. Went into a daze. What was your
> question?
>
>   DETECTIVE VINCE
> Who was the man in the mask?
>
>   SPARROW
> Some guy. Don't know who he was or why they
> kidnapped him, but Robert kept calling him Bob.
> Must be a fascination for guys to name things after
> themselves.
>
>   DETECTIVE VINCE
> You and Zack work together?
>
>   SPARROW
> Didn't see him much. He works in the I.T.
> department. You know how they are locked
> away in their computer cyber space world.
>
>   DETECTIVE VINCE
> Don't you think that's a coincidence.
>
>   SPARROW
> Robert and I met when we where searching for a
> CD by Snow.
>
>   DETECTIVE VINCE
> Snow?
>
>   SPARROW
> A Canadian rapper who sings reggae.
> What a coincidence.
>
>   DETECTIVE VINCE
> When they came in to take someone out, you snapped.

75. INT. APARTMENT LISA BEDROOM DAY

Sparrow does not have a gun. Cole stands next to her, ready to make his move.

Chandler is holding on to Robert with the gun at the back of his head.

> LISA
> Sparrow for crying out loud, drop the gun!

> CHANDLER
> One.

> ROBERT
> Remember when you asked if I loved you.

> CHANDLER
> Two. Might I remind you that all I need is the masked man.

> ROBERT
> If you love me, put the gun down.

Chandler cocks the gun.

> CHANDLER
> Three.

> SPARROW
> Alright.

Chandler releases his grip on Robert, he keeps the gun pointed at the hostages.

> CHANDLER
> Your girlfriend was smart. Go downstairs.

Robert and Lisa walks slowly and make there way out of the room.

> CHANDLER
> Robert, Lisa, follow me.
> (talking to Cole)
> Tie her up, take her to the other room.

Chandler slams the bedroom door.

Zack removes his mask.

> ZACK
> Why did you take my mask off?

> COLE
> It doesn't look right If you have your mask on the

entire time. You're a hostage.

Cole looks at Sparrow.

                        COLE
Sparrow scream so it sounds like I'm beating you.

                      SPARROW
Aaahhhh!!!

                        COLE
Good. I'm going to find Chandler, make the calls.

                      SPARROW
I will.

Cole leaves the room.

                        ZACK
Want me to go with you?

                      SPARROW
No. Stay in here and rest. You did your job.

                        ZACK
Do you feel like you're getting   stiffed by Chandler.
I don't trust him. He's worth so much money.
What's his motive? What's his reason? Did you
know he's asking his dad for two million dollars.

Sparrow leaves the room.

                        ZACK
    (to himself)
We'll see how much money I get once I start talking
to the cops.

76. INT. APARTMENT HALLWAY NIGHT

Sparrow is on the outside of Lisa's bedroom. She hears Zack talking to himself.

                    SPARROW
    (to herself)
Chandler was right about Zack.

77. INT. APARTMENT SPARROW'S BEDROOM NIGHT

Sparrow returns to her room.

She dials the phone.

> SPARROW
> Everything is going as Planned.

78. INT. INTERROGATION ROOM DAY

Sparrow and Detective Vince are talking. They are drinking bottled water.

> DETECTIVE VINCE
> Where you and Zack in the same room while this was going on.

> SPARROW
> No they moved me.

> DETECTIVE VINCE
> You saw their faces.

> SPARROW
> No. I saw Zack's face.

> DETECTIVE VINCE
> What happened next?

> SPARROW
> They tied us up again, put blindfolds on us and took us downstairs.

> DETECTIVE VINCE
> Each of you have a different story to tell.

> SPARROW
> How? We where there together.

> DETECTIVE VINCE
> I should say from different angles.

> SPARROW
> Is that all Detective?

> DETECTIVE VINCE

>   For now. We're hoping that Zack comes out of his
>   mild coma. He had an allergic reaction to
>   peanuts. Know anything about that?
>
>   SPARROW
>   Pity.

The Detective stands, Sparrow does the same.

>   SPARROW
>   If I can be of any assistance.
>
>   DETECTIVE VINCE
>   Before you leave, there's' one last thing.

79. INT. OUTSIDE OF INTERROGATION ROOM DAY

Sparrow sips from her water and walks past Detective 1 who gives her a nod.

DETECTIVE 1 FLASHBACK

80. INT. INTERROGATION ROOM 2 DAY

Zack is waiting in the room.

Detective 1 walks in with a can of pop.

>   ZACK
>   It's about time.

Zack gulps down the pop.

>   ZACK
>   What's with the glove, afraid you might catch
>   something.

Zack falls on the floor.

Detective 1 puts some peanuts in his pocket. Detective 1 walks out.

Detective Vince walks in.

>   DETECTIVE VINCE
>   Mr. Hunt?

81. INT. APARTMENT LIVING ROOM DAY

TITLE OVER:

                    TWO DAYS LATER

Chandler's wife, SYLVIA REMMINGTON-VILDERMAN, Sparrow, Cole, and Cole's wife are in the living room.

Sylvia has the money in an attaché case.

                        SYLVIA
            Where's Lisa and Robert.

                      SPARROW
            Lisa is with her parents, Robert went home to pack
            for our trip.

                      COLE
            Who are you?

                      SPARROW
            Chandler's wife. Mrs. Sylvia Remmington - Vilderman.

82. EXT. RIVER DAY

Cole ties Zack.

                      CHANDLER
            Zack stay here. The police will be here in no time.
                      ZACK
            Do you have to hit me?

                      CHANDLER
            Its has to look realistic.

Cole punches Zack a few times.

83. INT. DETECTIVE 1 OFFICE DAY

Detective 1 is wearing gloves he rubs peanut oil on top of the pop can.

84. INT. APARTMENT LIVING ROOM DAY

Television is on, Sparrow use the TV remote to turn the Television down.

                      COLE

>   Where's Chandler, and Zack?
>
>   SYLVIA
>   Zack is in the hospital dying from a peanut allergy.
>
>   SPARROW
>   Chandler said that Zack wanted the money for himself.
>   I heard Zack say he was going to turn us in.
>
>   COLE
>   Chandler had it figured...

Sylvia hands Cole a brief case.

>   COLE
>   Cole, this is for you.

Coles wife takes the brief case.

Cols wife respond.

>   COLE'S WIFE
>   Thank you.

Sylvia hands Sparrow a case.

>   SYLVIA
>   Sparrow this is for you. Dad knows you don't need it.
>   Money is his only way of saying thank you.
>
>   COLE
>   Why did you help us Sparrow? You have money.
>   I didn't know that.
>
>   SPARROW
>   I learned through Detective Vince that my father
>   died in prison. Left everything to me.
>
>   COLE
>   What about Zack's wife?
>
>   SYLVIA
>   She'll go free.
>
>   COLE
>   Where's Chandler?

SYLVIA

On the day of the incident he came home to tell me about what was going on. Then took off with some of Dad's money. Did he come back here?

SPARROW

No he didn't.

COLE

He returned with these two cases and left.

SYLVIA

My father want to purchase your Jamaican Villa.

SPARROW

It's his. It is beautiful. It sits high in the mountains, over looking the ocean.

SYLVIA

(to Sparrow)
My father thank you.
(to Cole)
Cole, what are your plans?

COLE

We are moving far from here, change our names, our social security numbers. I'm going to start a financial service.

SYLVIA

Good for you.

COLE

About your dad.

SYLVIA

Five years ago he gave my brother a hundred million dollars. He gave me one million.
Said, "women don't need that much Money.
I showed him.

COLE

But...

SYLVIA

You wife uncle is looking for her. Shouldn't you

leave.

                    COLE
          I was just saying.

News is heard from the television. Sparrow turns the sound up. They stop and listen to the news.

                    NEWS REPORTER
          This just in, a new development on the kidnapping
          case. The Columbus police discovered that
          Zack Hunt kidnapped himself, then blamed his wife
          of ten years for his kidnapping. Mrs. Hunt is going
          free this afternoon. However, her husband died a
          few hours ago. Zack ate some peanuts, a food
          group that he is highly allergic to. Detective Vince
          found his body on the floor in the interrogation room
          with peanuts in his pocket. The twenty-four hour
          kidnapping is over. But Detective Vince stated,
          "the case is under investigation." This is...

Sparrow turns the sound down.

                    SYLVIA
          Chandler had Zack killed.

                    SPARROW
          Zack was going to let his wife rot in jail.

                    COLE
          How did Chandler know about Zack?

                    SYLVIA
          Chandler told me, he heard Zack making plans.

85. INT. APARTMENT HALLWAY DAY

Chandler is standing at the top of the steps looking down at Zack talking on the phone.

86. INT. APARTMENT LIVING ROOM DAY

Sylvia and Sparrow are standing in front of the living room doorway.

                    SYLVIA
          We proved to dad that women have backbone.

When you called and said everything was going as planned, Chandler was there.

                         SPARROW
Where is Chandler? I don't buy he ran away.

                         SYLVIA
Dad hired a hit man. That's all you need to know.

                         SPARROW
Am I safe.

                         SYLVIA
Dad never liked Chandler. Chandler was trying to Take over dad's company. He was so involved, he never noticed that we were in control.

                         SPARROW
We make a great team.

                         SYLVIA
Dad gave the company to me. I am hiring you to take over Chandler's position.

                         SPARROW
I don't know what to say.

                         SYLVIA
Say you'll take it.

They shake hands.

The End.
CREDITS ROLL

CHAPTER SIX

Bonus Scenes

Scene 1

EXT. PARK – DAY

SPARROW and ROBERT are in a park walking and talking.

>   ROBERT
> A few nights ago, we were hostages.
>
>   SPARROW
> I am glad that's over.
>
>   ROBERT
> You okay?
>
>   SPARROW
> Yes. You did an excellent job pretending to be a victim. At one point, I thought Chandler was going to shoot you.
>
>   ROBERT
> In a sick way, that was a good thing.
>
>   SPARROW
> Yes it was he had no idea you were a part of it.
>
>   ROBERT
> Now we're free to leave.
>
>   SPARROW
> I have two more things to do. Will you Help?
>
>   ROBERT
> No problem.
>
>   SPARROW

Then, we're off to France. I have to make a stop in
Jamaica. I have a meeting with my mother's lawyer's.
I am getting the Villa, and my trust fund.

ROBERT

What are you going to do with the Villa?

SPARROW

Sell it.

ROBERT

At least you're getting away from Lisa.

SPARROW

I've grown weary of hearing how rich her parents are.

ROBERT

How did you meet her?

SPARROW

In church, her car was jammed with stuff. I asked
if she needed help. At the time her car was home.

ROBERT

Where are her parents?

SPARROW

In a small town, they kicked her out.
She forgot she told me.

ROBERT

Interesting.

SPARROW

I wonder what Lisa will say about the
the incident.

ROBERT

She will Say, I saved everybody, they could not
make it without me.

They laugh.

SPARROW
Are you sure you don't mind moving to France.

ROBERT
Moving don't bother me, I wonder how are we going to live. I'm a Korean American, you're an African who says she's from Jamaica, but claims to be an American. What bothers me, who are you?

SPARROW
I'm from West Africa, we speak French. Mom changed our birth certificate, dates we were born, our names, and our birth country. Then hide everything from dad. Mom was an attorney, so she knew what to do and how to get it done.

ROBERT
Really.

SPARROW
When war broke out in my country my mother's family escaped to France. To dodge my father, mom and I were to escape to America, then join our family in France. Dad moved us to Jamaica. I ran her.

ROBERT
You've been running every since.

Robert slows down.

ROBERT
Is Sparrow your real name.

SPARROW
It's the name mom gave me to use in Jamaica and America. In France I will go back to my original name. My name is Delight.

ROBERT
Delight?

Robert abruptly stops walking.

SPARROW
Robert, I am sorry for lying to you.

ROBERT (astonished)
Delight, Sparrow.

SPARROW
I like Sparrow. When we get to France
They will call me Delight.

ROBERT
Are you ever coming back to America?

SPARROW
Yes I like it here.

ROBERT
And my family is here.

SPARROW
Then it's settled.

Sparrow looks away in silence. Robert senses her sadness; he reaches into his pocket and pulls out a ring. He puts it back into his pocket.

SPARROW
Come on Robert.

Robert close the box, and catch up with Sparrow.

ROBERT
Tell me about the Villa.

They walk towards the stage.

SPARROW
It is beautiful it sits on a mountain over looking the ocean. It has an enormous porch, and big backyard. The house has sixteen rooms, and seven bathrooms. In a distance are the servants' quarters. They worked for my father. I wonder if they are still there.

ROBERT
Miss. Delight, when we get to Jamaica I have a surprise for you.

He turns facing her, gets a flower and places it in her hair.

> ROBERT
> You are to me what Josephine Marcus was to Wyatt Earp.

Sparrow steps back and bow from waist down.

> SPARROW
> You are my Wyatt Earp, together forever. Is that us?

They continue to walk.

> SPARROW
> What's the surprise? Why wait?

> ROBERT
> Your running days are over.

> SPARROW
> That's not the surprise, although it's a good thing.
> No more running.

Robert is playful with sparrow as they continue to walk.

> ROBERT
> What is our next project?

I saw a British movie where the scene was being shown, over the scene was the actors talking then they walked past camera into the scene.

Scene 2

INT. FRANS PLACE – DAY

SPARROW and MAVIS are Visiting FRAN.

>   FRAN
> I am through with your roommate what's her name.

>   SPARROW
> She's okay at times.

>   MAVIS
> Other times she's a pain in the butt.

They laugh.

>   SPARROW
> Fran thanks for getting the info on Zack. Mavis thanks for watch duty at the park.

>   MAVIS
> Usually not that many people is in the park.

>   FRAN
> It's always like that.

Sparrow gives the women an envelope

>   SPARROW
> Here's a little something for your help.

The women examines the envelop.

>   MAVIS
> I was not expecting this much. Twenty dollars would have done it for me.

>   FRAN
> Girl, lunch.

They laugh.

>   FRAN
> Sparrow, I am going to tell my brother about you. I told him you're a beautiful black woman who need

>   a brother by her side.
>   (looks at Mavis)
>   Don't you agree?
>
>   MAVIS
>   No I don't. Stay out of Sparrow's business.

Fran stands and goes to the kitchen.

>   FRAN
>   I want to help the sister out. I mean because what
>   she's dating...
>
>   MAVIS
>   Fran, shut up! Sorry, she runs her mouth way too much.
>
>   SPARROW (whispers)
>   It's okay.

Fran enters the sitting area with a tray of ice tea.

>   FRAN
>   I have ice tea for us.
>
>   SPARROW
>   You shouldn't have gone through all the trouble.
>
>   FRAN
>   It was no trouble. I also made finger sandwiches.

Fran leaves.

>   FRAN (from the kitchen)
>   Sparrow, my brother is a lawyer, after this mess
>   you may need one. He's handsome and single.

BEAT

Sparrow is not happy, Mavis reach for a glass. Sparrow shakes her head no.

MONTAGE:

Sparrow reach in her pocket and pulls out rubber gloves and a shower cap. Mavis does the same.

From the kitchen, we hear pans falling on the floor.

Sparrow and Mavis sit and wait.

Tracy comes into the room.

                          TRACY
            It's done.

Sparrow and Mavis begin to clean.

The chairs, dust the floor

                          MAVIS
            She couldn't shut up.

                          SPARROW
            Can you keep a secret?

                          MAVIS
            I have always kept secrets.

                          SPARROW
            Good.

They continue to clean.

                          MAVIS
            With the money you gave me, my son and I are
            going to live well.

                          SPARROW
            Leaving the company?

                          MAVIS
            No, I am going to get my masters in computer science.
            Move up in the company.

As Tracy hands Mavis an envelope she looks into her eyes.

                          TRACY
            Take this.

Mavis looks confused.

                    SPARROW
        It's Fran's cut.

                    TRACY
        Mavis you can leave. You job is complete.
        You did good.

Tracy walks with her to the door, Tracy has a plastic bag and towel.

Tracy lays the towel on the floor.

                    TRACY
        Remove your shoes, gloves, and plastic cap,
        place them in this bag.

                    MAVIS
        What will I wear home?

Tracy hands her a pair of socks.

                    SPARROW
        Sorry Mavis, Tracy is a woman of few words,
        but she's very thorough.

                    MAVIS
        With the money you gave me, I can purchase
        as many shoes I want.

She removes her shoes, gloves, and shower cap, then drops them in a bag. She leaves.

INT. FRANS KITCHEN - DAY

Tracy finishes dusting the floors. Sparrow takes the tea dishes into the kitchen and begins to wash them. Fran is lying dead on the kitchen floor, with a gun lying on her abdomen.

Tracy enters the kitchen, the dust mop is in a plastic bag.

                    SPARROW
        Who's gun.

                    TRACY
        Her brothers, funny he keeps a gun in his desk
        drawer. People need to lock their stuff up.

                    SPARROW (light laughter)
        Tracy, am I safe with you around.

							TRACY
				(smiles for the first time)
					You're cool. Besides Mr. Remmington would
					never put a hit on you.

Robert knocks at the back door.

EXT. INT. FRANS PLACE KITCHEN – DAY

ROBERT'S POV

Sparrow answers the door she is happy to see him, Tracy is in the background.

							SPARROW
					Robert!

He starts to enter, Sparrow reaches for him. Tracy steps between the two.

							TRACY
					You'll have time for that later.

Tracy gives the bag with the mop to Robert. She drops the dishcloth, drying towel in the bag.

							SPARROW
					Why are throwing those away.

							TRACY
					They will have your DNA on them.

							SPARROW
					My head, hands were covered.

							TRACY
					Not this part of your arm.

Sparrows arms are wet.

							TRACY
				(to Robert)
					Know where to take these.

							SPARROW
					Where is he taking it.

TRACY
I know a guy at one of the local dumps he runs the incinerator.

ROBERT
Can't we throw it away?

TRACY
What do you think?

ROBERT
Fire will destroy the...

TRACY
Sparrow, where did you park?

SPARROW
Five blocks away. I came in the front door.

TRACY
We're leaving out this door. Wait here.

She goes inside. Pulls a broom out of a bag and begin to sweep, back and forth. Sparrow closes the door.

ROBERT
Our last night in America is not the way I though
it would be.

Tracy comes out carrying stuff, she place them in the plastic bag. She hands the bag to Robert.

SPARROW
Why were you sweeping her floor?

TRACY
The broom was new, it didn't have Fran's DNA
or apartment debris. I'm leaving the Broom and dustpan.

She removes her shoes.

ROBERT
(to Sparrow)
I will pick you up later.

                    TRACY
        That is taken care of, your flight is a red eye.
        Robert someone will pick you up, Sparrow someone
        else will pick you up.

                    SPARROW
        Are we leaving on the same plane?

Tracy looks at both Sparrow and Robert.

                    TRACY
        Your clothes are being packed as we speak. They
        will be shipped to the Jamaican Villa. A smaller
        case will be left behind for you to carry.

                    ROBERT
        It will look like we're going on a vacation.

Sparrow removes her shoes. Davis does the same; they place them in the bag Tracy is holding.

                    TRACY
                (to Sparrow)
        I'm driving you to your car. You two are not
        to see each other until you're in the airport.

                    ROBERT
                (to Sparrow)
        See you there.

He leaves with the plastic bags.

MONTAGE:

The empty sitting room is neat and tidy.

Kitchen is clean. On the floor lies Fran. With a gun on her abdomen, hole in her throat, a small stream of blood has rolled down her cheek onto her neck.

EXT. FRAN PLACE PARKING LOT - DAY

Tracy and Sparrow standing by the car.

                    TRACY
        Ready for to nights meeting?

SPARROW
I'm going home shower, put my hair in a pony tail.

TRACY
Mavis cannot be trusted.

SPARROW
Why?

TRACY
Her eyes, she's lying.

Sparrow looks blank. They get into the car and pull off.

SPARROW
When?

TRACY
When you're on the plane.

SPARROW
Cole?

TRACY
I have a person watching him.

SPARROW
Robert?

TRACY
He lives.

We had so much fun shooting this scrip. Who-would-have-thought, eight pages to film and just as many bloopers.

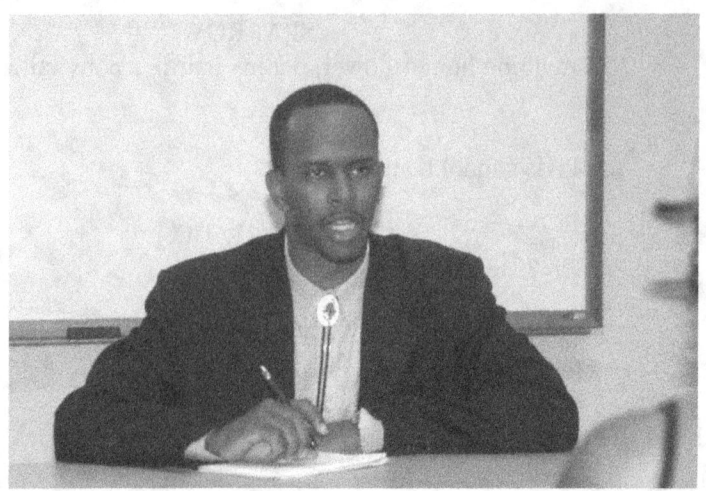

Detective Vince (Ricky) getting to the truth.

Scene 3

EXT. SPARROW, LISA, MAVIS, FRAN IN FRANKLIN PARK - DAY

Sparrow, Mavis, and Fran walking in the park, when Sparrow sees Lisa running towards them.

                SPARROW
Hi Lisa.

                LISA (out of breath)
Sorry for being late, I have so much to do today. I am always so busy. I thought you wanted to see only me, who…

Mavis and Fran watch Lisa in disbelief, than at each other.

                SPARROW
Lisa meet Mavis and Fran, coworkers of mine, Fran, Mavis Lisa, my roommate.

                LISA
I know she tell you bad things about me, but leave out that her boyfriend is over all the time.

Mavis and Fran looks vacantly at Lisa.

                MAVIS
She-she said that you were planning a costume party.

                SPARROW
Why don't you like Robert?

                LISA
It takes time from us, I want to talk, watch a movie, talk about people, my job and ignorant supervisor. Now you bring them.

                SPARROW
We can talk to night.

                LISA
Sounds good, just us two and nobody else, right? When is Rob coming over?

SPARROW
I bought a movie for tomorrow night. He's coming over then.

LISA
See, more Robert.

SPARROW
Let's discuss our costume party.

LISA
You mean your costume party, which is a month away. Why discuss it this early?

SPARROW
Why procrastinate?

LISA
No matter what I suggest, you always do something else.

MAVIS (disgust)
Sparrow do you have a theme?

SPARROW
Not yet, I was thinking…

FRAN
60's or a 70's party.

MAVIS
The seventies was a wild and crazy time, hippies, flower power, afros, and black power.
    (she hold up a fist)

FRAN
I am going to wear an afro wig.

SPARROW
I'll come as a 70's version of Cleopatra.

LISA
Today I'm getting my hair done, I'm going with blond extensions. What do you think Sparrow?

FRAN
Don't see you as a blond.

LISA
I was talking to Sparrow.

SPARROW
It matches your personality. Lisa looks very pleased
with Sparrow's response.

Sparrow walks over to the Santa Maria sign and read.

SPARROW
Music. O'Jays, Spinners, Platters…

Sparrow walks back to the bench and sits down.

Lisa begins to sing Fats Domino song, Blue Berry Hill.

LISA
I found my thrill, on Blue Berry Hill.

MAVIS, FRAN & SPARROW
Sing girl.

LISA
SINGS THE NEXT LINE

MAVIS
Lisa you should be a singer.

SPARROW
I keep telling her that.

LISA
My parents are not like yours, they would have a fit…

SPARROW
What do you know about our parents?

LISA
I assume that you all were born in poverty, parents
not…Sparrow listens tentatively. Mavis walks
over to Lisa, tight fist, teeth clenched.

MAVIS

You know nothing about…

LISA
Unlike me, my parents are lawyers,
they have money.

Mavis takes a swing towards Lisa. Sparrow grabs her hand.

SPARROW
Why are you staying with me? Get your own place.
Remember how we met?

FRAN
You insulted me, I will call a lawyer and sue you.

Sparrow looks at Fran.

MAVIS
I don't have to take this.

Mavis leaves. Sparrow shakes her head at Lisa and follows Mavis.

MAVIS
You're good, I would have kicked her out a long
time ago.

As Sparrow and Mavis walk away Lisa glance at the women with rage. Fran storms away.

SPARROW
The costume party is her farewell party. She don't know it.

MAVIS
You should tell her tonight, maybe that will bring
her down a notch.

SPARROW
I like the element of surprise.

Fran running towards Sparrow and Mavis

FRAN
Wait for me!

We shot this scene in Franklin Park, but the sound inside Esther's apartment. It was a fun scene to shoot and oh so beautiful, the sun was shinning bright, the leaves were multi colors of yellow, orange, red, brown, and a hint of green.

It turned out to be an absolute mess, it was added to the bloopers section. I chalked it up as experience.

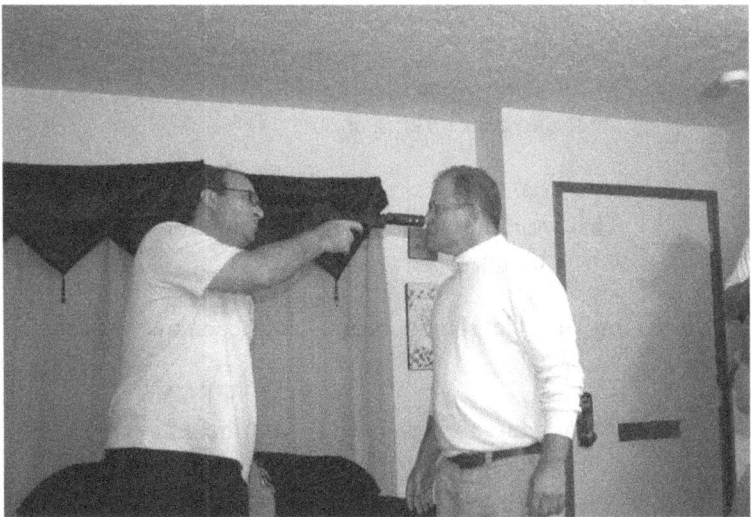

Kidnappers turn on each other. (John and Ned)

Scene 4

INT. INSIDE PORCH – EVENING

SPARROW is meeting with an associate of Remmington's Company and TRACY in her Aunt, MRS. DAILEY, home.

                SPARROW
Mr. Divercy thank you for meeting me here, I feel safer. No ears lurking about.

                TRACY
That would not happen I would monitor everyone's where about.

Mrs. Early brings out a tray of juice, she pours and hands each one a glass.

                MR. DIVERCY
Thank you for letting us use your home.

                MRS. DAILEY
No problem.

                SPARROW
Auntie, meet Mr. Divercy an associate of the company, and Tracy our computer programmer. Mr. Divercy, Tracy, meet Mrs. Dailey.

                TRACY
You treat Sparrow very well.

                MRS. DAILEY
I saw her sitting in a shopping mall Crying - We talked – I learned that she was alone, we adopted her into our family.

                MR. DIVERCY
That was nice of you.

                MRS. DAILEY
She's a good girl, once a week she takes me out to lunch.

Mrs. Johnson turns to leave.

                MR. DIVERCY

Everything is going as planned.

                SPARROW
Are you going to tell Remmington's daughter about Chandler?

                MR. DIVERCY
I'll let him tell her.

                SPARROW
Think the officer will report us?

                MR. DIVERCY
It's rare when a cop gone bad tells anything. Extra money is good. We're safe.

                SPARROW
        (to Tracy)
Chandler keeps an extra gun in a wall cabinet behind his desk.

                TRACY
Is it locked?

                SPARROW
No. Just in case, I taped a key under the coffee table in his office.

                MR. DIVERCY
        (to Tracy)
What time are you meeting him?

                TRACY
Tomorrow, before going home he strolls in the park at three o'clock.

                MR. DIVERCY
        (to Tracy)
Do you have the oil?

                TRACY
Yes.

Tracy hands Sparrow a bag.

                MR. DIVERCY

(to Sparrow)
The detective is meeting you by the transportation building. If he's not there or if he's with Detective Vince you're not to approach them. Call Tracy.

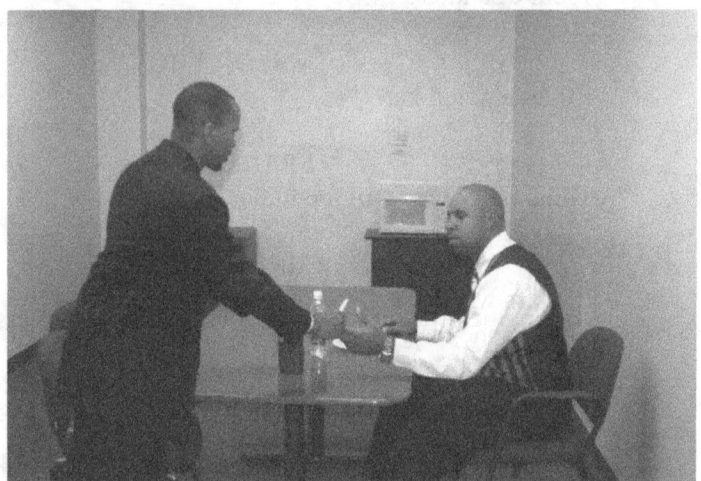

The two Detectives (Ricky and Bill) going over evidence.

Scene 5

EXT: PARK – DAY

MONTAGE:

CHANDLER is walking on the companies' park trail.

We see Chandler looking around from TRACY's POV.

He gets suspicious when he hears a noise behind him.

He turns around and sees nothing.

Tracy the hit man discretely follows him.

He turns again; Tracy goes into the woods.

We see Chandler through the trees from Tracy's point of view.

Tracy comes out of the woods, Chandler turns around, we see Tracy from Chandler's POV.

Chandler is startled.

                        CHANDLER
            Don't you work with Zack?

BEAT:

Tracy walks closer to him.

                        CHANDLER
       Shouldn't you be at work? Lunch time is over.

She continues walking towards him. She slowly pulls out the gun.

                        CHANDLER
            What are you reaching for?

Chandler begin to back up.

                        TRACY
     Mr. Vilderman, Mr. Remington sends his regards.

                     CHANDLER (nervous)
     Whatever he's paying you I will pay you more.

BEAT:
>   I'm the one who made the company what it is.

We hear the construction crew machines.

> CHANDLER
> People will hear the gunshots.
>
> TRACY
> Your construction crew will mask the noise.

Tracy continues to walk towards Chandler. She aims the gun.

Chandler freeze.

Tracy shoots Chandler in the middle of his brow.

Chandler falls dead.

Tracy walks away.

EXTRA SCENES:
The extra scenes was inserted through out the movie, the original ending with Sparrow on the phone remained the same.

Once the third editor completed the editing, the film was a little over sixty minutes. He suggested that we go back into production. Several of the original actors returned to complete the movie.

It took two weeks of pre-production and one week of production.

CHAPTER SEVEN

Below is the scene count according to the page. Each page in a screenplay is divided into eighths. This will help with figuring out approximately how long the movie will be on screen. Also, this will help when planning the shooting schedule.

		page			page			page
Scene	1	3/8	Scene	30	3 3/8	Scene	59	2
Scene	2	2/8	Scene	31	1 1/4	Scene	60	2/8
Scene	3	5/8	Scene	32	2 3/4	Scene	61	5/8
Scene	4	1	Scene	33	6/8	Scene	62	2/8
Scene	5	1/8	Scene	34	2/8	Scene	63	6/8
Scene	6	1/8	Scene	35	2	Scene	64	2/8
Scene	7	1/8	Scene	36	1 1/2	Scene	65	1 7/8
Scene	8	2/8	Scene	37	2/8	Scene	66	7/8
Scene	9	1/8	Scene	38	3/8	Scene	67	5/8
Scene	10	1/8	Scene	39	1 1/8	Scene	68	1 3/8
Scene	11	2 7/8	Scene	40	3/8	Scene	69	1 3/8
Scene	12	1 1/2	Scene	41	4/8	Scene	70	7/8
Scene	13	1 3/4	Scene	42	2/8	Scene	71	1 1/2
Scene	14	5/8	Scene	43	1 3/4	Scene	72	3/8
Scene	15	1 3/8	Scene	44	1	Scene	73	1 3/4
Scene	16	4/8	Scene	45	2/8	Scene	74	2/8
Scene	17	2 3/4	Scene	46	3 5/8	Scene	75	6/8
Scene	18	6/8	Scene	47	1 1/4	Scene	76	1 1/4
Scene	19	3 1/4	Scene	48	3/8	Scene	77	2 1/8
Scene	20	5/8	Scene	49	6/8	Scene	78	1/8
Scene	21	7/8	Scene	50	1 1/8	Scene	79	2/8
Scene	22	2 1/8	Scene	51	1/8	Scene	80	2 1/8
Scene	23	4 1/4	Scene	52	2/8	Scene	81	1/8
Scene	24	5/8	Scene	53	5/8	Scene	82	6/8
Scene	25	4/8	Scene	54	2/8	Scene	83	3/8
Scene	26	3/8	Scene	55	2/8	Scene	84	4/8
Scene	27	6/8	Scene	56	2/8	Scene	85	1/8
Scene	28	2 1/8	Scene	57	4/8	Scene	86	2 3/4
Scene	29	4/8	Scene	58	3/8			

Actor Call Sheet

Here is an example of the call times for the main actors during the initial shooting. "nn" means not needed.

Chandler Vilderman

John Michaels

Day	Time In	Time Out
Thursday 9-14	nn	nn
Sunday 9-17	8:00am	6:30pm
Monday 9-18	6:00pm	9:30pm
Tuesday 9-19	6:00pm	8:00pm
Wednesday 9-20	7:00pm	9:30pm
Thursday 9-21	6:00pm	9:30pm
Sunday 9-24	8:00am	7:00pm

Sparrow Jenkins

Esther Madison

Day	Time In	Time Out
Thursday 9-14	3:15pm	5:00pm
Sunday 9-17	8:00am	6:30pm
Monday 9-18	6:00pm	7:30pm
Tuesday 9-19	nn	nn
Wednesday 9-20	6:00pm	9:30pm
Thursday 9-21	7:00pm	9:30pm
Sunday 9-24	8:00am	7:00pm

Robert Lee

David Lim

Day	Time In	Time Out
Thursday 9-14	9:30am	1:00pm
Sunday 9-17	9:30am	4:30pm
Monday 9-18	6:00pm	9:30pm
Tuesday 9-19	nn	nn
Wednesday 9-20	6:00pm	9:30pm
Thursday 9-21	6:00pm	9:30pm
Sunday 9-24	8:00am	7:00pm

Lisa Bennett

Miesha Cannaday

Day	Time In	Time Out
Thursday 9-14	1:45pm	3:30pm
Sunday 9-17	nn	nn
Monday 9-18	nn	nn
Tuesday 9-19	nn	nn
Wednesday 9-20	6:00pm	9:30pm
Thursday 9-21	6:00pm	9:30pm
Sunday 9-24	10:15am	7:00pm

Cole Harris

Anthony Henderson

Day	Time In	Time Out
Thursday 9-14	nn	nn
Sunday 9-17	8:30am	4:30pm
Monday 9-18	nn	nn
Tuesday 9-19	6:00pm	8:00pm
Wednesday 9-20	7:00pm	9:30pm
Thursday 9-21	nn	nn
Sunday 9-24	8:00am	7:00pm

Zack Hunt

Ned Lynch

Day	Time In	Time Out
Thursday 9-14	4:45pm	6:00pm
Sunday 9-17	8:00am	6:30pm
Monday 9-18	6:00pm	7:30pm
Tuesday 9-19	6:00pm	8:00pm
Wednesday 9-20	6:00pm	9:30pm
Thursday 9-21	7:00pm	9:30pm
Sunday 9-24	9:15am	7:00pm

Detective Vince/Asst Director/Writer

Ricky R. LaVaughn

Day	Time In	Time Out
Thursday 9-14	7:30am	7:00pm
Sunday 9-17	7:30am	7:00pm
Monday 9-18	5:00pm	10:00pm
Tuesday 9-19	5:00pm	10:00pm
Wednesday 9-20	5:00pm	10:00pm
Thursday 9-21	5:00pm	10:00pm
Sunday 9-24	7:30am	7:00pm

Detective 1

Will Cunningham

Day	Time In	Time Out
Thursday 9-14	4:45pm	6:00pm
Sunday 9-17	nn	nn
Monday 9-18	6:30pm	9:30pm
Tuesday 9-19	nn	nn
Wednesday 9-20	nn	nn
Thursday 9-21	nn	nn
Sunday 9-24	nn	nn

CREW

Day	Time In	Time Out
Thursday 9-14	7:30am	7:00pm
Sunday 9-17	7:30am	7:00pm
Monday 9-18	5:00pm	10:00pm
Tuesday 9-19	5:00pm	10:00pm
Wednesday 9-20	5:00pm	10:00pm
Thursday 9-21	5:00pm	10:00pm
Sunday 9-24	7:30am	7:00pm

CHARACTER NAME	Scene Number	Total Number of Scenes	Number of Speaking Parts	Speaking/ Scene
Chandler Vilderman	1, 2, 3, 4, 5, 6, 7, 8, 9, 10, 14, 15, 19, 23, 27, 28, 30, 32, 35, 46, 47, 49, 50, 51, 52, 53, 59, 63, 65, 67, 68, 69, 71, 72, 73, 74, 77, 83, 84, 86	40	190	4.75
Sparrow Jenkins	1, 3, 4, 5, 6, 7, 8, 9, 10, 11, 13, 15, 17, 19, 21, 23, 30, 35, 39, 41, 43, 44, 46, 59, 61, 62, 63, 64, 65, 66, 68, 69, 70, 71, 72, 75, 76, 77, 78, 79, 80, 81, 83, 84, 86	45	198	4.40
Robert Lee	1, 3, 4, 5, 6, 7, 8, 9, 10, 11, 12, 13, 15, 16, 17, 18, 19, 20, 21, 23, 27, 28, 30, 32, 35, 36, 38, 39, 40, 41, 42, 43, 44, 45, 46, 47, 48, 49, 50, 51, 52, 53, 54, 56, 62, 65, 67, 75, 77	49	153	3.12
Lisa Bennett	2, 3, 4, 5, 6, 7, 8, 9, 10, 13, 15, 17, 19, 21, 22, 23, 24, 26, 27, 28, 29, 30, 31, 32, 33, 35, 39, 41, 43, 46, 47, 49, 53, 65, 67, 75, 77	37	122	3.30
Cole Harris	1, 3, 4, 5, 6, 7, 8, 9, 10, 15, 19, 21, 23, 30, 32, 46, 47, 53, 59, 63, 65, 66, 68, 69, 73, 77, 83, 84, 86	29	116	4.00
Zack Hunt	1, 3, 4, 5, 6, 7, 8, 9, 10, 13, 14, 15, 19, 23, 27, 30, 39, 41, 46, 57, 59, 63, 65, 69, 73, 74, 75, 77, 82, 84	30	73	2.43
Detective Vince	12, 16, 18, 20, 22, 24, 25, 26, 29, 31, 33, 34, 36, 37, 38, 40, 42, 45, 48, 54, 55, 56, 57, 60, 61, 64, 70, 76, 80, 82	29	117	4.03
Detective 1	25, 34, 37, 55, 57, 60, 81, 82, 85	9	1	0.11
Cole's Wife	83, 86	2	1	0.50
Zack's Wife	19	1	0	0.00
News Reporter	49	1	1	1.00
9-1-1 Operator	2	1	1	1.00

How I Produced A Movie With Eight Thousand Dollars

10:00 - 6:00	8:30 - 6:30	6:30 - 9:30	6:30 - 8:00	6:30 - 9:30	6:30 - 9:30	8:30 - 7:00
Thursday 9/14	Sunday 9/17	Monday 9/18	Tuesday 9/19	Wednesday 9/20	Thursday 9/21	Sunday 9/24
library	apartment	shelter house/park	apartment	apartment	apartment	apartment
12	56	54	5	13	2	14
16	67	82	6	29	27	71
18	1	47	7	73	34	87
20	11	49	8	43	38	3
35	41	48	9	75		4
37	59	52	10			15
39	63					17
42	65					19
45	69					21
51	74					23
53	77					31
55	66					40
22	70					44
24	72					46
26	76					50
28	85					60
30						62
32						64
58						81
61						84
68						86
78						
25						
33						
36						
57						
79						
80						
83						

Thursday 9-14

10:00am - 1:00pm	12, 16, 18, 20, 35, 37, 39, 42, 45, 51, 53, 55
1:00pm - 2:00pm	Lunch
2:15pm - 3:30pm	22, 24, 26, 28, 30, 32
3:45pm - 5:00pm	58, 61, 68, 68, 78
5:15pm - 6:00pm	25, 33, 36, 57, 79, 80, 83

Sunday 9-17

8:30am - 9:30am	56, 67
10:00am - 11:00am	41, 11
11:15am - 12:15pm	1
12:15pm - 1:15pm	Lunch
1:30pm - 4:00pm	59, 63, 65, 69, 74, 77
4:30pm - 6:30pm	66, 85, 70, 72, 76

Monday 9-18

6:30pm - 7:15pm	54, 82
7:45pm - 8:30pm	47, 49
8:45pm - 9:30	48, 52

Tuesday 9-19

6:30pm - 8:00pm	5, 6, 7, 8, 9, 10

Wednesday 9-20

6:30pm - 7:00pm	13
7:30pm - 9:30pm	29, 73, 43, 75

Thursday 9-21

6:30pm - 7:00pm	2
7:30pm - 9:30pm	27, 34, 38,

Sunday 9-24

8:30am - 9:30am	14, 71, 87
10:00am - 10:45am	81, 84, 86
10:45am - 11:45am	17, 40
11:45am - 12:45pm	23
12:45pm - 1:45pm	Lunch
1:45pm - 2:45 pm	19, 62, 64
2:45pm - 3:30pm	31
3:30pm - 4:00pm	21
4:00pm - 4:30pm	60
4:30pm - 5:00pm	15
5:15pm - 5:45pm	44

5:45pm - 6:15pm	46, 50
6:15pm - 7:00pm	3,4

Main Scene	Detail	Area	Time	Scene Numbers
Abandon Playground		Int	Day	54, 82
Apartment	Backyard	Ext	Day	5, 6, 7, 8, 9, 10
Apartment	Hallway	Int	Day	66, 70, 72, 85
Apartment	Hallway	Int	Night	76,
Apartment	Kitchen	Int	Day	14, 71, 87
Apartment	Lisa Bedroom	Int	Day	2, 27, 29, 34, 38, 73
Apartment	Lisa Bedroom	Int	Night	43, 75
Apartment	Living Room	Int	Day	3, 4, 6, 8, 10, 13, 15, 17, 19, 21, 23, 62, 64, 81, 84, 86
Apartment	Living Room	Int	Night	31, 40, 44, 46, 50, 60
Apartment	Sparrow Bedroom	Int	Day	1, 63, 65, 74
Apartment	Sparrow Bedroom	Int	Night	11, 41, 59, 69, 77
Car		Int	Night	47, 49
Detective 1 Office		Int	Day	83,
Interrogation Room	Lisa's Scene	Int	Day	22, 24, 26, 28, 30, 32,
Interrogation Room	Robert's Scene	Int	Day	12, 16, 18, 20, 35, 37, 39, 42, 45, 51, 53, 55
Interrogation Room	Sparrow's Scene	Int	Day	58, 61, 68, 78
Interrogation Room	Zack's Scene	Int	Day	80,
Outside Interrogation Room		Int	Day	25, 33, 36, 57, 79
Park	Outside Office	Ext	Day	56, 67
Street		Ext	Night	48, 52

Wardrobe list for main characters.

character name	wardrobe meeting day	wardrobe day of incident AM	wardrobe day of incident PM	wardrobe interrogation day
Chandler Vilderman	business	business casual	same clothes business casual	casual
Cole Harris	business	business casual	same clothes business casual	casual
Zack Hunt	business	business casual	same clothes business casual	same clothes business casual dirty
Sparrow Jenkins	business	night clothes	casual	casual
Lisa Bennett		night clothes	casual	casual
Robert Lee		night clothes	casual	casual

Detective Vince				suite
Detective 1				suite

Producing a film is hard work there is the lack of sleep, body run on fumes, short tempers, constant planning and thinking, keeping up with where everyone should be, and the time they are to be there. Included in this list is the unbelievable hard job of staying within the budget. Yet, being on set is absolutely the best time of my life, the icing on top is watching the finished product in a theater with total strangers and watching their reaction. What a rush.

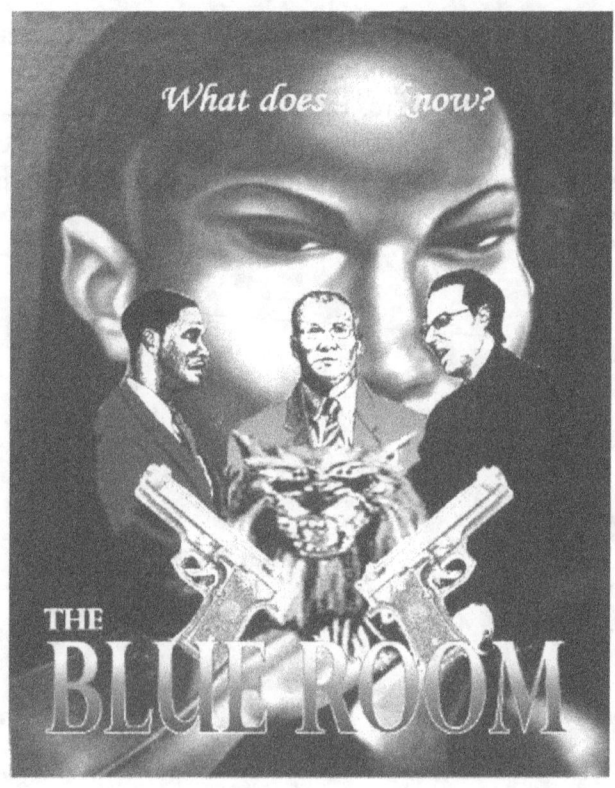

Artist designer William E. Knott, Jr. created the picture to be the marquee; it drew people to the theater to see "The Blue Room."

Visit www.lavonproductions.com for more information on the film "The Blue Room."

If you think it, believe it, just do it, then enjoy the benefits of getting it done. Bravo.

Sandra L. LaVaughn

www.ingramcontent.com/pod-product-compliance
Lightning Source LLC
Chambersburg PA
CBHW080457220526
45465CB00006B/2299